The Country Beyond

JANE SHERWOOD

The Country Beyond

SAFFRON WALDEN
THE C.W. DANIEL COMPANY LIMITED

This edition was first published in Great Britain
by Neville Spearman Ltd
in 1969
Re-published by The C.W. Daniel Company Limited in 1991
1 Church Path, Saffron Walden
Essex, CB10 1JP, England

ISBN 0 85207 254 6

'The Country Beyond' was first published in 1944.
The present edition contains the original work together
with additional material from an earlier book,
'The Psychic Bridge'.

The Random House Group Limited supports The Forest Stewardship
Council (FSC®), the leading international forest certification organisation.
Our books carrying the FSC label are printed on FSC® certified paper.
FSC is the only forest certification scheme endorsed by the leading
environmental organisations, including Greenpeace. Our
paper procurement policy can be found at
www.randomhouse.co.uk/environment

MIX
Paper from
responsible sources
FSC® C018072

Printed and bound in Great Britain by Clays Ltd, St Ives PLC

Set in 11pt Baskerville 3 pt leaded.

Introduction

I had the great privilege of meeting Leslie Howard twice before his untimely death. We met first by appointment to talk about my first book, *The Psychic Bridge* and on this occasion Mr. Howard took home with him the as-yet-unpublished MS. of *The Country Beyond*. He read the MS. and offered to write a preface for it. His journey abroad and its tragic ending prevented the carrying out of this intention.

His interest in the problems raised was profound. His keen and sensitive mind was searching and forming tentative conclusions about the many theories advanced by spiritualist writers. He said: 'It is not so important that people should make up their minds about these things as that they should be presented to them in such a fashion as to command respect from serious-minded men and women. So much of this type of literature is based on wishful thinking and exploits the bizarre and sensational. I myself do not regard any of these things as proven but I am aware that there is a mass of evidence, to cover which no adequate theory has been advanced. We are less than honest if we shut our eyes to this evidence. Moreover, materialistic theories are proving less and less satisfactory to thoughtful people and the time has surely come when we must look to science to outgrow its prejudices and to get to work in earnest on the field which is being opened up by psychic research.' In the course of further conversation he said: 'I believe that we are on the verge of great discoveries in the realm of mind and books like this may well act as stimuli to the launching of a new hypothesis of matter

5

which will bridge the gulf between the materialist and the spiritualist. Who knows,' said Mr. Howard in a burst of optimism, 'perhaps in years to come we shall be saying "Do you remember how it all began?" '

Much of the material given to me in the communications that follow was abstruse and difficult in its first forms. It cannot, I think, be simplified beyond a certain point. I have tried to clear it of confusion and to state it clearly. Over-simplification is too often falsification and the problem my Communicators have had to face has been the presentation of complex truths in such a way that they should not be distorted by my ignorance.

My hope is that the reader will use this book, as Leslie Howard suggested, as a starting point from which to begin his own research. The thoughts given to me have many implications which could not be worked out by me, notably the pregnant suggestions about the nature of time. Ideas are fascinating, vital, potent things; they can take a bewildering variety of significant forms according to the soil in which they grow. My hope is that the seed I am helping to sow will bear its own characteristic harvest in the minds of others and that the final form of truth in their minds may differ from that in my own. In such differences lies the hope of the future. I trust, therefore, that the reader will not accept my truth but will use it as a means to obtain his own.

When I first began to experiment I was warned by those who had experience that there were certain dangers which might have to be faced if one opened one's mind to influences from the spirit world. It was suggested that not all influences were good and that mischievous ones were constantly seeking to work upon mens' minds. Since I was ignorant of the conditions into which I was seeking to enter I did not take these warnings seriously; in fact, I scoffed at them as morbid and superstitious. So I had to buy my experience dearly and am anxious to pass on the warnings to would-be experimenters.

For the dangers are real and they are of two kinds. It is unfortunately true that there are earth-bound spirits of mischievous tendency who can and do interfere with the records and falsify communications by misleading suggestions. This is a danger which should be recognised by any experimenter. It is particularly likely to occur during the early stages of his development. The danger is minimised if goodwill and helpfulness are felt for these unfortunates. It is obvious, after all, that both good and evil men must die and that their surviving personalities will continue to do after their kind. The work of re-clamation of such unfortunates goes on all the time but is sometimes a long and difficult task for those devoted souls who give themselves to this work.

The second danger comes from within and is far more to be feared. One goes into this search for truth for many reasons perhaps largely because of a vivid intellectual curio-sity. One is apt to overlook the fact that one's moral qualities are of the highest importance. During the de-velopment of psychic powers there are changes in the scope and kind of consciousness when great emotional upheavals seem inevitable. The unconscious mind is, as it were, stirred to its depths and all manner of repressed contents come flooding up into consciousness causing experiences so fan-tastic, so agonisingly over-charged with emotion that it is very hard to keep one's mental balance and one often hears of sad cases where this crisis has been fatal to stability. A trained and disciplined mind and body, with emotions purified and controlled are necessary to the psy-

7

chic experimenter. He needs a high degree of courage to face the unknown since experiences in this kind are always unique and so cannot be prepared for in advance. But courage itself is not enough; it may well add to the dangers. Only a stabilised character can afford real protection against the hazards of such an enterprise.

For it is in effect a deliberate attempt to anticipate the next stage of human evolution and the breaking through of a new power of living always endangers the balance of the old. I knew none of these things and so ran into serious danger. I had to adjust to a new focus of attention while my whole world was rocking in a storm of emotions. That I came safely through the dangers was largely due to the loving understanding of my three friends who steadied and guided me through this difficult time. They are the entity known as 'Scott', my husband, Andrew, and an older and wiser friend known by his initials, E.K. The story of how I made contact with them is told in the early part of this book. There are certain emotions which I found to be especially dangerous and at all costs these must be recognised and brought under control before one dares initiation. In my own case a violent and selfish sorrow, unaccepted and resented, yet outwardly repressed for many years had now to be released in waves of agony under which I died many deaths. I had to learn acceptance and humility before I found any relief from this suffering. Then, alas, I had never succeeded in controlling an impatient temper. Now I had to learn that anger endangered all those who came near me, no matter to whom my impatience was addressed. If any of my friends approached me at such times their sensitive bodies were seared by my anger and when I at last realised that they suffered thus for my fault I tried hard to learn better control. I came to realise, too, that indulgence in any

8

unworthy emotion laid me open to influences of the same unworthy nature, a kind of justice I did not enjoy. As my own body became more sensitive I too learnt what it meant to be literally burnt by waves of hatred or anger and had thus convincing proof of the near-physical nature of the emotional being.

Other discharges of feeling became known to me in their true nature. Fear, the most fundamental of all emotional disorders, created around me a heavy miasma from which my friends hastily withdrew. They described such conditions as 'a gas attack' and somehow I needed to master fear if they were to remain near me. Even when fear has, one thinks, been tracked to its roots he would be a reckless man who declared that he had plucked it completely out of his being. It can only be mastered, it seems, by the habit of mind which can throw itself overboard, can lose its life to save it and dares to take all that comes in the spirit of love and acceptance. This, I fear, involves a life-long discipline.

To understand even in part the lessons my friends tried to teach me I had to become docile and teachable, to empty my mind of preconceptions and pride and to become as a little child. This did not mean that I was absolved from using my reason; far from it. My friends used it for me and so poor an instrument was it that years of training were necessary before it would think their thoughts or carry their meanings. Every power of the mind is needed in this work and a vacant or ill-trained mind limits if it does not deform the truths which it should transmit. The medium is an instrument and the better the instrument the better the work that can be done with it.

Lastly, keeping the balance between the two worlds of experience is no easy task. Double vision does not make for steady walking. At first, under the impact of powerful new experiences, practical affairs fade in importance and one is inclined to neglect them, for all the things of the senses take on a dreamlike quality and yet may at times be lit up with intense meaning and beauty. Familiar faces, familiar scenes take on a startlingly new aspect. Disconcerting glimpses of the mysterious reality behind physical appearances come unawares upon the mind and are as suddenly lost again. Nothing remains constant to its old appearance and an unruly crowd of new impressions are superimposed upon the ordinary world of the senses. It is as though the level ground upon which one had always walked confidently had taken to heaving up in waves beneath one's feet. The double vision, the two-fold experience has to become habitual before one can walk without stumbling. During this difficult period of adjustment E.K. constituted himself my guardian and guide. Bewildered and often astray I was glad to take his automatic control in practical matters. Quietly I was led here and there, my movements nicely calculated so that I met this person, or avoided that. My hand was guided to the book I needed to read and even the words that I must speak were put into my mouth. This lesson of docility was difficult, but in my need I learned it thoroughly. When the need passed and I was more at home in my two-visioned world automatism was no longer practised.

I cannot enough emphasise the warning that automatism is exceedingly dangerous unless one can trust one's guide implicitly. *Even then, the conscious standards of right and wrong, the ordinary laws of suitable behaviour must control the situation at all times.* Otherwise, one has no guarantee that the unconscious mind itself is not the controlling agency and in this case one's proper place is a mental home. The conscious mind must *never* allow its own standards to be overruled.

To sum up, then, the qualifications of the psychic experimenter. He should be a man of balanced and serene mind who has been able to purify and control his emotions; he must be humble and docile and yet willing to use every power of intellect and vision to the full; he should have a well stocked mind since the shortcomings of the instrument will limit its usefulness. Above all, he must cast out anger and shame by way of acceptance for he has to learn to live in a world where nothing can be hidden, where every subterfuge of thought and every undesirable feeling has to be acknowledged. He has to accept himself with all his weakness and guilt without wasting time and strength in vain self-justification or excuse. This is not an easy standard to reach but failure to reach it will bring its own nemesis. The mystics insisted on a period of training they called purgation before allowing their disciples to begin on the stages of initiation. Those who essay personal research in psychic matters need a no-less arduous novitiate.

Chapter One

THE SEARCH

Stubbornly my mind reviewed the facts. There had been Andrew, most virile and energetic of men, his young and healthy body super-charged with life; there had been his letters, full of ardour and instinct with his loving, optimistic personality. Then a silence, a shattered body somewhere in France and the rest—simply gone, they would have one believe. Each cell and molecule growing cold, disintegrating and yielding up its elements to the mould. Just a question of matter, energy, fields of force dispersed. How did these things account for the sum of power, of lovely, subtle form which made up a human being? Granted that every shred of matter could be traced to its home in the earth again, could that matter carry away the whole sum of energy of a man? What about the conservation of energy? The theory didn't seem to work here.

I saw Andrew wielding an axe, felt the wind of the stroke and heard the crash of the blow that cleft the oak; thought of him as he tore down the football field concentrating his full weight in a kick that carried the full length of the field; thought of the patient processes of thought, the steady output of mental energy, recalled his flashing fun and the irresistible contagion of his gaiety. Where was it all? Conservation of energy—it simply didn't work. What, then? He was not. You couldn't count that broken body out in France and I refused the blasphemy of the rest—'For God took him' which was to confound the Almighty with a German shell or its factory-driven maker, or with the inspirer of the policy which made use of such things. No, God had not taken him. To whatever resignation dope in religion you subscribed, it would not cover that. Man had taken him—lunatic, fear-driven man. I waited for the anger and dismay of this conviction to pass and tried again to grasp the impossible equation. Take the sum of a man, subtract his shell of matter driven by chemical energy and the answer is a cipher. Man—chemical energy = nothing. Nonsense. Reason revolted and declared the equation false.

What had religion to say about it? It collected from the grave a thin wraith—a soul, whatever that might mean and bore it off to some attenuated heaven where it led a blameless paradisal life, shorn of all its weaknesses and failings, of all its hunger for good earthly joys and satisfactions. Rather sudden, that transition, I thought. I realised, almost with a chuckle, Andrew's probable reactions to the harp and golden crown. He would want work and plenty of it, he would need to get his teeth into things, to organise, to shoulder responsibility and feel the satisfaction of tasks well done. And if I knew him at all, he would be yearning over those left behind and would find no rest while they sorrowed. Could all the ethereal joys of heaven make him forgetful of lost hopes and broken ambitions, cut off before their flowering? It would have to be a very distant heaven and a very different Andrew to adapt to such conditions. I didn't think it likely that human beings could change so radically and so suddenly as that. No, if he persisted at all he persisted with much the same character. After all, what was to change him? A sudden shock, pain, bewilderment at a new order of things? These would work no real change in a man's make-up. I reflected on the slow years of experience needed to modify any trait of character, of the slowness of 'Growth in grace' as my puritan parents would have put it. I thought of Andrew's faults. In my eyes he had very few, but I was not such a fool as to think that in the testing of everyday married life we should either of us have proved flawless. No, if he persisted it was as a personality very little changed and therefore no likely denizen of a bland and bodiless heaven.

If he persisted, I thought; if he, Andrew, had real existence in this real world I was exploring in thought. Why, what was the room and the firelight and the table at which I wrote? They faded out into nothingness, meaning had gone out of them and I was out in the great universe of real being searching for Andrew and, more than that, convinced that he was there. That meant that the long years of beating in vain on the blank wall of death were over for me. It wasn't a blank wall blocking out all hope for evermore. As I groped it thinned out into a fog, a dark ocean of unknowing, but in it walked the lost and sorrowing forms of men.

That gripped me, because I knew that he *would* be sorrowing. Why, would even I have gone on my shining way regardless if he had been left behind, broken and alone? What if the strong tide of grief that shook me was not my own alone, but his also? I panicked at this and almost wished he might be safe in some remote heaven. He was perhaps groping in this same fog for me. Unbearable. We were doubling our sorrow, two energies of suffering acting simultaneously on both of us.

Could any effort of mine find him? God, how I had tried! Felt for him, spoken to him, reached out in an agony of longing, waited in suspension of being for response in any form. And there was nothing. The conviction grew that this had been his frustration and despair as well as my own. If I could entertain this possibility how could

I possibly sit down under it in hopelessness, or was there any way of piercing this wall of separation, now worn so thin? Mediums claimed the power to speak with the dead, even to see them. What was this power and had they a God-given monopoly of it? Were their pronouncements genuine or was it always fraud, self-deception, a form of hysteria? But how could one judge without knowledge and how did one set about to investigate such claims? Was it possible that such powers were common to us all but in differing degrees of development?

'What a piece of work is man'—and surely far more than an organised system of chemical energies. Yet something must be lost with the chemical shell if it was only the peculiar 'Bodiness' of a physical being. But if there was a beyond-body being incorporated in each of us then I also was more than the sum of my chemical energies. So to make contact with this beyond body of another, one must learn to use the corresponding body in oneself. Could some way be found to put the fleshly being by so that the voices of these others might become audible to the inward ear and their thoughts pass into the inward mind? I had already, as I thought, evidence that their emotions could be felt in spite of the shrouding flesh. I needed a method of recording in some definite fashion what was at present only dimly felt.

Thus I fumbled, strongly suspicious of wishful thinking, floundering among half-understood concepts and stray echoes of pseudo-science. I cursed my inadequate education yet realised that scientific training resulted more often than not in a bigotry of materialism as intolerant as the religious bigotry it replaced. All research along conventional lines seemed to reach the same frustration. 'Here we are at the end of the path, a good and proper path, ruled straight by logic, paved by good intentions and fenced with integrity and yet it leads nowhere.' What next? Only platitudes about human limitations.

I thought of all the keen intellects, the trained minds that had actually made the transition into the unknown. If they could only pass back accurate observations on which to base some theory of the change itself they would surely be able to indicate the link between their state of being and ours. Moreover, they could make the necessary comparisons with their old knowledge and carry the analysis of energy on a further stage. Then where were they, these men of genius and good will? Did they know of our predicament and realise the dangerous insanities to which mankind was descending and from which their knowledge might save us? They must surely be as anxious to reach us as we were to receive trustworthy evidence of their existence.

I thought I knew my world with its almost abject faith in science. There were murmurs to be heard, hints here and there that men were awake to values not included in a scientific methodology. But for the ordinary man the scientist had become the High Priest of truth, his every word sacrosanct. In the name of science men were asked to accept far more baffling mysteries than any religious faith had demanded of them and they accepted them unquestioningly. If knowledge of this other world was to find general acceptance it would have to be linked with science and carry scientific authority. No ethical or philosophical sanction would suffice nowadays.

But these were daydreams and I came back to my own position amidst the dim probabilities that I could discern. All that was possible for me to do was to use them as assumptions and as a basis for experiment. I should need to read and study the experiences of others and train myself to share them if it proved that I had the ability. I should have to discount the fear of self-deception and take any risks there were with my eyes open. At the least it would be a psychological experiment; at the best I might glimpse some objective reality. At this stage my ignorance and my optimism were equal. I had very little appreciation of the dangerous path to which I was committing myself nor the long and arduous journey I had still to make.

I had reached this decision when an odd circumstance befell. I was spending a holiday with a friend of my younger days whom I seldom saw. Her mother was an enthusiastic Spiritualist and we discussed her faith. I tried to push the discussion into more speculative regions and got a totally unlooked for response. 'I have been a long time hesitating,' my friend said, 'before telling you about a message which came over some months ago at a seance I attended with Mother. I was not taking part and sat outside the circle. The medium insisted that there was a message for me from a soldier. I was reluctant to be involved and told her that I had no friends in the Forces. She urged that the message was urgent but that it was not for me personally but for a friend I should soon be meeting. As you know, you and I had neither met nor written for two years so you were a long way from my mind and at first I was at a loss. Now I am wondering if it could have been meant for you.'

My friend had written down the detailed message when she received it and now handed me the paper on which it was written. The message was clear enough. A soldier wished to make contact with his wife and to assure her that he was often with her. So far, safe generalities, but it went on to details which were only too applicable to my present circumstances and which showed clear knowledge of all that had happened to me since Andrew's death, many things of which my friend could have had no idea. At first any critical judgement of the message was impossible; it came too near home. All my theorising had been driven by strongly repressed emotion and at this intimate response I was shaken out of all composure. It was as though, fumbling blindfold in that fog of uncertainty a hand had suddenly clasped mine to assure me that I was not searching alone. I excused myself and went off alone.

Presently I tried to assess the real value of the message. It gave clear proof of knowledge of my doings and reassured me on points where I might have doubted Andrew's approval. It seemed to me entirely typical of him and if I could trust it, of great importance to my peace of mind. How much of this information could have been got from my friend's mind? She had a general knowledge of my circumstances but the long gap in our intercourse made it unlikely that she should have conveyed even that much to the medium. Then there were the significant details of which she had never known. I was of course, entirely unknown to the medium and the other sitters. There seemed a fair chance of authenticity.

Then I began to speculate on the means by which Andrew had come to use this very unlikely connection. He had known my friend slightly but would have no reason to connect her with Spiritualism. And how came he to know that after such a long interval we should renew contact? I checked on that—the advance had come, not from her but from me. I had suddenly found myself thinking of her, had guiltily realised my neglect and had written asking her to meet me. From this meeting had come plans for a joint holiday. Was all this coincidence or a deliberate impressing of my mind by Andrew? Had he got that communication through to her and then set to work to direct my thought to my friend and so bring his own prophecy of our meeting to pass? I reviewed our common friends and realised that this was literally the only one among them with any contact with Spiritualist circles and so the only possible channel through which a message could have reached me.

This began to wear the air of a deliberate attempt to communicate. There was evidence of an organised effort, thorough and patient, which was entirely characteristic of the man. I could only guess at Andrew's part in all this and the obstacles he had had to surmount. The show of probability tantalised me because I could only see one half of the process. I was still fighting a losing battle against the sceptical side of my mind and I ruefully admitted that such a strong desire to believe might invalidate judgement. But I had to consider not certainties but possibilities if only out of loyalty to Andrew and the effort he may have made to reach me. After all, if I was fooled, or fooled myself, no one was the loser but myself; if I refused to make any attempt to respond I failed him. Commonsense in this context might well be cowardice. So the challenge must be accepted; I would assume that the message was genuine and would set to work to find out whether contact with him was possible. Thus I pledged myself to a fateful journey into queer byways of human experience, a detour away from accepted paths, at times a difficult and dangerous one, but always excelling in interest and adventure the safe highway of commonsense.

Private speculations were one thing but I lacked the means of testing them. I decided first to explore the claims of recognised Spiritualism. I began to attend Spiritualist meetings and to read their literature. I found myself faced with a confused mass of assumptions and claims and had to suspend judgement until more of this extraordinary material was collected. There appeared to be a structure of theory arising among a confusion of fantastic scaffolding which travestied its form. Credulity working on dream and marvel and the more sensational happenings of the seance room had reared this inconsequential surround. One had to ignore this jungle if the solid nature of the building rising within was to be seen. I was repelled by the starry eyed credulity and by the marvels it fed on but I became aware that some logical theory was being built behind all this jungle growth.

The fantastic element was my chief stumbling block. I heard much talk of Red Indian Guides, Child Guides, Egyptian and Chinese Guides but seldom or never of English Guides. Why should these outlandish trappings inspire such complacency in the breast of both medium and sitter? Was it childlike love of the weird and fantastic or was there some genuine reason for it? Some controls spoke through their mediums in broken English or in the accents of childhood and the unlikeliness of Chinese or Egyptian speaking in English at all, broken or otherwise, did not seem to occur to anyone. The messages were often of extreme banality, trivial and platitudinous, but on the other hand they were uniformly kind and probably helpful in effect. Communications varied from the kind that advised the sitter to wear a certain colour because it matched his aura to others of a high ethical standard. Attempts at personal messages from friends and relatives who had 'passed over' were seldom in convincing form and those that came to me usually took the form of a pretty gesture of handing me a bunch of symbolic flowers or of vaguely reassuring prophecies of future well-being. Nothing could

21

have been further from my need. I was full of urgent questions about the why and wherefore and was not to be fobbed off by this kind of moonshine.

Spiritualist periodicals were of various kinds—highbrow and earnest, popular and sensational or frankly crude with a direct appeal to the superstitious or morbid. A good deal of space was given to seance room miracles, 'apports' or 'materialisations', messages purporting to come from great ones recently dead. These latter were saddening since they were seldom on the level of intelligence one expected from their alleged authors. I had to admit that I knew nothing of the process involved and that its difficulties might prevent characteristic transmissions. There were long articles on esoteric mysteries in the better class of periodicals and discussions on theosophical and mystical subjects. The correspondence columns reflected much credulity and muddled thinking; terms were used in wild confusion and many of them were in the strange jargon which had grown up about the subject.

Spiritualist books were bewildering. Substantial theories were propounded but a lush emotional atmosphere hung about most of these descriptions of the life of the blessed. There was more than a hint of Mr. Chadband in some of the teaching. Then there was the unmistakable influence of eastern esotericism. Gleaming marble temples built in ancient symbolic form and served by oriental priestesses were often the instruments of observance of a glorified Church of England rite. Descriptions of towns had the same fairytale quality of gorgeous pageantry subject to surprising invasions of angelic visitors from higher spheres. It seemed to me a perfervid hotch-potch of mystery and imagination gleaned from romantic and esoteric sources and left me faintly hostile and suspicious. There was very little of the drastic attempt to understand the conditions of this new life and their connections with this present one of which I was in search. One needed bread and was given, not a stone, but custard pie. Eventually I came upon the books of Rudolf Steiner. Here at last I was offered a coherent theory. The picture here presented was of a series of levels of being the ascent of which was made as one became capable of living in them and this notion of gradual progress satisfied the need for a logical process of growth and development. One was told, too, that on the lower of these planes the environment took a form very similar to that of earth and that life went on in bodies which appeared to their owners as substantial as our own. The form of matter on each plane thinned out as one ascended and the descriptions of higher planes grew correspondingly vague. There were references to dimensional differences in time and space which suggested a possible connection with scientific thought. Along with this went cosmic theories of which no proof was offered. They had to be taken as the inspired knowledge of one whose spiritual development made him capable of seeing and knowing them in an extra-sensory way.

I attended Spiritualist meetings. At the best type of gatherings a prominent place was given to the study and exposition of the Bible as a record of little-understood psychic phenomena. The person of the Christ was usually presented as that of a super-medium. There was apparent a genuine attempt in all this to link the spiritualist movement with orthodox Christianity. The speakers at such meetings were earnest and sincere, but the climax of these gatherings, whether of this or a less sophisticated kind, was the final half-hour given to mediumistic communications. The medium was the magnetic centre of the gathering. A fearful intentness was felt as the messages were given and the strained expectancy of all made for a strongly emotional atmosphere, weighted with sorrow and hope. The messages were usually personal, trivial and platitudinous but they must have satisfied the eager hope of those to whom they were given.

The mediums with whom I came in personal contact were of several kinds. Some few had the power to transmit images of beauty and significance and this power was not confined to those of better education. One in particular I recall whose appearance and accent were of comfortable vulgarity and yet she gave her messages in the form of beautiful and significant pictures which seemed to be helpful and appropriate to the needs of her sitters. There were others who with closed eyes and pious mien produced nothing but wearisome platitudes, others who in their private utterances gave painful exhibitions of spite and self-advertisement. No message was ever received by me from Andrew under these conditions so I decided to try private sittings.

I was told many strange things in the course of these. Sometimes they seemed to consist of repeated efforts to recall little known and distant relatives. The medium would ask: 'Did you once know someone named Anne or Annie?' I search my memory and dredge up vague recollections of a second cousin by marriage and reply cautiously 'Well, yes I did but it's a long time ago.' I am then given a message from Annie who certainly would not know me now if we met in the flesh and can hardly be expected to retain the slightest interest in me. I am, in fact, surprised to find how many of my long-dead relatives wish to communicate with me now when during their lifetime they hardly knew of my existence. As to Andrew, I am told that he is sometimes present but only on one occasion does his presence bring with it any emotional impact. On this occasion I am strongly affected by a condition of charged emotion and there is no mistaking the difference in atmosphere between this and the other sittings. The medium does not seem to be affected by it but my temples are oppressed by a sensation of heavy pressure and I leave the sitting cold and trembling. During this sitting I find myself catching the echoes of a voice. I hear questions and answer them mentally. I am asked the reasons and aims of my quest and I reply asking for enlightenment and help. Then the medium takes up the word and fails to continue or amplify what I think I have been hearing. The inevitable question occurs: did I create this situation out of my own desire and were those near-physical sensations, inner voices and response just so much hysteria? Or, if they were genuine how was it that the medium remained deaf to it all? Or again, was it possible that she and I, sitting together in the same room, could make different contacts at the same time? As my experiences continued this uncertainty was always present, a drag and hindrance to any progress yet not to be ignored for fear of the credulity born of desire.

On another occasion a message was given which troubled me. A man, who might well have been Andrew by the description given, was present. The medium said: 'He is showing me a rope that has been knotted twice, one knot over the other. He is loosening the upper knot and when that is untied it will be easy to free the other. He says it will be like that with you and that he is helping you to untie the first knot.' This had a dangerous application to difficulties in my own life which I had scruples about removing for myself. It had the effect of bringing into consciousness a possibility that I did not feel right to put into action. I had no impression of the power and presence which had made the other sitting memorable and the dangerous nature of the message gave me pause. Thinking it over afterwards, I concluded that this was a good example of the 'telepathic' message. Conflict in my own mind had been read and exteriorised by the medium who was probably quite unaware of the source of the mental image she had passed on.

I felt I was getting nowhere. The chances of an authentic message appeared to be remote and I was becoming very impatient of all this irrelevant triviality. I needed to find a medium of sterner mould, but if I told her in advance what kind of contact I was looking for, how should I know that something of the kind would not be deliberately produced for me? It seemed hopeless to find a medium who could or would honestly use her powers in such research and I concluded that I should not find one among professional mediums.

In my desperation I began to entertain seriously the idea of developing some kind of mediumistic power myself. Lacking this, all information had to be taken at second or even third hand and my faith in professional mediumship had been severely shaken by my experiences. Only through one's own mediumship would one be able to come to honest conclusions. The risks would then be reduced to two: self-deception, and the unreliability of the intelligence with whom one appeared to be in contact. Serious risks, and not to be eliminated by any amount of care and caution. Self-deception, as much as this could be guarded against, must be checked by vigilant self-scrutiny, but the second risk had to be taken as the price of further experience. If I got any response I could not put down to my unconscious mind I should at least have a foot on the lowest rung of the ladder. If it were possible honestly to regard it as experimental proof of the existence of discarnate intelligences the actual experience might convert mere belief into knowledge. By now, I was hungering and thirsting for certainty.

The torment of doubt, desire and hope deferred had become unbearable.

I knew something now of the ways in which mediumistic power might be developed and trained. In several communications received through a medium I had been urged to attempt to take automatic writing and though I believed that I had heard and followed mentally the spoken word on at least one occasion I felt that this might be an uncertain and perhaps dangerous method; writing would inspire far more confidence. It would also permit reperusal and criticism of what came through. It was asserted that such writing could be produced from one's own unconscious mind and of course, this objection could be made against any form of mediumship. The only safeguard and that a partial one, would be a critical assessment of content and style. First develop the power and then begin to worry about the results, I thought. Prejudging the case would get me no further. There were two methods: one was to sit quietly and wait for impressions to come into the mind and then to record them immediately. This, I thought was likely to give the unconscious mind a free pass into expression. I remembered knots and double knots and shrank from this method. The other way was to sit with pencil poised and wait for automatic movement as though the pencil moved of its own volition. This would be very thrilling but hardly probable. The practical question of how a disembodied entity could move so many grammes of wood and lead without any help from my muscles was quite insoluble at that stage of my development. But I would not be discouraged from experimenting and such questions could be left until I got results, if this ever happened. So I set to work.

I began sitting alone in a quiet room. My mood was sceptical in self-defence, but acutely expectant for all that. I had gathered that it was advisable to empty the mind of all content and lay it bare for the reception of impressions. I conscientiously attempted this but found it a discipline that required much practice and was never fully successful. My attempts usually finished in a concentration on the thought of Andrew and the hope that I might again feel his presence. But I remained alone in a void. There was nothing. I tried sitting with pencil poised in a none-too-steady hand with my wrist raised from the paper. The pencil occasionally quivered and I was certain that I had not initiated any movement. Once it traced a shaky line across the page, but nothing intelligible appeared. Tiring of protracted failure in this method I tried again clearing my mind and recording words or phrases which came into it unbidden. Perhaps a word, perhaps only a letter would start into consciousness and I hopefully wrote it down. Still nothing of significance ever appeared. My obstinate resolution kept me faithful to such efforts for a space of two years without any real success. In the course of these years I also tried to develop clairvoyance. One thing might perhaps help the other and I could return to the writing method if I had any success.

The attempt to 'see' was also beset with difficulties. Attention was distracted by the persistent return of memory pictures and when these were banished patterns and colours of flickering light would play on the curtain of the closed eyelids. I persevered and thus became conscious for the first time of the phenomenon of 'hypnagogic hallucinations'. This portentous title is given to visions which occur on the verge of sleep and are often strikingly life-like. They were often beautiful and seen clearly in vivid colour and I found that they also had the power of progression as movement and development followed the original vision. Varied and unpredictable as they were, they had one thing in common; they were completely unrelated to anything seen or known by me. The people who appeared in them were all strangers; the scenes were unfamiliar and they had no relevance to the conscious content of my mind. They were fascinating, but unhelpful and when I began to enquire about them I found that they were a well-known and common experience.

All these early and tentative experiments were interesting but I could usually find psychological explanations for all the results. I was so baffled by the conviction of 'aloneness' that went with them. I knew with certainty that there was no one at the other end of the line so to speak, and was irrationally astonished and hurt by the silence and lack of response. This was naïve to a degree but it illustrated the strength of my expectancy and gave me the negative consolation that I was unlikely to invent a response on account of that expectancy. This comforted me in a wry fashion but left me at a loss as to my next effort.

I was living near a large seaside town and one day it occurred to me to go in search of a Spiritualistic church. I was directed up squalid backways and finally shown the way by a collarless man in a white shirt buttoned in one place only with a crystal stud which blinked at me with a sinister air. He sniggered at my question and turned to watch me across the road. Disquieted and ruffled I nearly gave up the attempt but found the church at last up a hidden alleyway and made my way in. I was reassured by a sunlit and cheerful interior, flowers on a rostrum and a sound of distant singing from the rear whence a caretaker emerged. I was told that a seance was to be held that afternoon and I decided to stay and attend it. All the details of this seance are very clearly in mind because it had far-reaching results. At the moment my disagreeable search had left me in a far from receptive mood and I watched a small group assemble with a critical eye. There were ten of us, varying from a poorish housewife to a couple who turned out to be a doctor and his wife.

The medium worked by means of psychometry, that is, she handled personal belongings of each of the sitters as she gave her messages. The contributions from the audience were collected on a tray in advance so that the medium, as she took them up haphazardly had no clue to their ownership. I did not understand the method and in my sceptical mood the tray full of rings, brooches and small articles fingered by the stout, unmodish woman with her eyes shut and lips intently pursed seemed simply a grotesque piece of hocus-pocus. My turn was long in coming so I had time to reverse this judgement and to marvel at the aptness of the messages the medium gave. How did she divine the catholic faith of the quiet man to whom she imparted an appealing vision of a dim ecclesiastical interior filled with flowers and saints? He wore no emblem but acknowledged his faith and seemed glad of her message. Another, a determined looking business man, she described truly as an investigator far from convinced of her powers. The same queer intuition was apparent when she spoke to the housewife and assured her that 'her shopping basket would never be empty'. When she came at last to my token, a notecase that had belonged to Andrew, she showed no knowledge of this connection but immediately gave my occupation correctly. Then came a pretty message from an aunt recently dead and a cheering prophecy about the sunlit path of my future and the helping hands held out from the spirit world to aid me over what she described as a rough and stony pathway. Then I was told that there was one present who desired to help and guide me. I wondered if I was at last to make the desired contact with Andrew but was completely put off by the subsequent description. I was told that there was a person in a white robe an end of which he was holding across his face as though for a disguise. He was amused by her reference to his nose which was described as long and beaklike which he corrected to 'aristocratic'. The medium added that she thought he was an Egyptian and that he was anxious to help me to understand hieroglyphics and to know of the ancient mysteries of his land. This was the fantastic guise in which I had least sympathy with spiritualism and though I liked the sense of humour shown by my would-be-friend in the white robe I came away not much cheered.

Soon after this I made the acquaintance of a woman who was a table medium: that is, she took messages by the tipping of a table which thus indicated letters of the alphabet. I attended one of her sittings and was surprised at the power with which the table appeared to be rocked and the speed with which a message could be put together. Hearing of my efforts she suggested lending me a planchette, a triangular piece of wood about the size of an outspread hand with a hole at one end for the insertion of a pencil. It ran on two small ivory wheels and the hand was placed lightly palm downwards on the board. Any movement was registered by the pencil as it moved over a sheet of paper. I remembered how my own poised pencil had shown signs of independent activity and thought that this device might help in overcoming the inertia of the hand. She placed the toy on the table and rested her hand on it. With a slight creak of its wheels it moved up the table and then stopped. I thought that unconscious pressure must have been applied but when I tried it myself it was uncanny to feel the determined jerk with which it responded. I had heard of such gadgets before as adjuncts to a parlour game and had a vague theory about magnetic influence from the hand, but I took the thing home with me and that evening, as soon as I was alone I took a large sheet of paper, drew a circle on it, placed the letters of the alphabet around it and started to experiment. One placed the pencil at the centre of the circle, put one's hand gently on the rest and waited for signs of movement. Almost at once it stirred and began to walk across the paper and as it reached a letter I noted it down and replaced the pencil at the centre. I was intrigued and curious and persevered although that first evening I failed to get any significant grouping of letters. On succeeding evenings I tried again sometimes getting series that made words but these were only stray and meaningless. Then one evening on scanning the record I saw that one set of letters had recurred several times and the thought came to me that they might be initials. 'G F S' meant nothing to me. I could think of no one for whom they might stand. But when next I tried the planchette the mysterious letters recurred twice more and I paused, puzzled and at a loss. I again put the pencil to the centre and this time it walked right out of the circle and wobbled about on the white paper outside. This had never happened before and with the utmost care lest I deflect its course I relaxed my hand until it scarcely touched the wood. The pencil moved into a series of recognisable letters. They made a name, a signature— 'G. F. Scott'.

Curiously, not a doubt assailed me that an actual identity was represented by that signature. Its very unfamiliarity was reassuring. I had my response at last but from an unknown source. There was the seal of certainty about it, impossible to doubt. I knew that the first part of my search was over and after the years of lonely experimenting the shock of success halted me wordless. I felt, too, the impact of an emotion, a surprise and joy that matched my own. But who was this stranger?

For a while I could do nothing but sit back and wait for the realisation of this to quieten and steady. Then I took another sheet of paper and set the planchette free to write what it would. Writing came slowly at first and with anxious care I steadied and relaxed my hand feeling the letters forming underneath though I had to move the frame aside to read them. The writing was large and sprawling but quickly became more legible and the stupid little ivory wheels creaked and stuck under the effort to force them into faster action. Again and again a flood of relief and joy stopped the busy pencil and seemed to fill the room where I sat, no longer alone but strangely aware of an unknown friendly presence as though this stranger had indeed quietly walked into the silent room and was making himself known to me.

Chapter Two

I was aware from the first of a well-marked, robust personality and of a knowledge and ability far exceeding my own. Impressions of the appearance of this stranger came to me in many subtle ways. A curious way of 'seeing' him developed. When he was present I felt a reflection on my features of his expression, almost as if his face had been superimposed upon my own. I have since thought that this was again a matter of accurate thought-transmission; we all have an inner impression of our own faces and it was this that was transferred to me. I was strongly affected by his moods: amusement, impatience, gaiety and even anger were impressed in almost physical sensation in my body. His mind flashed strange, rich images into mine and his memories, fruits of a wide and adventurous life enriched my own dull experiences. This sharing of thought had its embarrassing aspect and I had to make a consciously exerted effort to 'cut the connection' when either of us needed to turn to other interests. Unaware sometimes that Scott had turned away, I sometimes caught snatches of talk not meant for me at all and had hastily to shut the door of attention. I was at this time quite unused to living simultaneously in two worlds and was finding the experience rather shattering. I had to accept the openness of my thoughts at any time and this, to a normally reserved and secretive nature was severe discipline. Complete candour was forced upon me and as a corollary, the reluctant facing of some unpleasant facts about my own nature. I learnt by degrees to take my punishment with some equanimity and to cease to hide from discreditable memories. I learnt also that my emotions had effect upon Scott since he assured me that when I felt shame and remorse for these things he simply had to go away until I recovered. So the exchange of emotions was obviously two-way.

I was aware that this companionship was strengthening and enriching my mind. To fit the experience into the usual psychological theory I should need to claim all this as my own, as a sudden and extraordinary mental development, a kind of late flowering of a quite commonplace mind. It was difficult to find in my own very ordinary experience any source for the richly textured memories which were being opened to me and which delighted me so much because of their unexpectedness. It was significant, too, that whenever I began to think out this theory of self-origin I had to encounter anger and reproach from Scott. On the whole, it was less of a strain on credulity to accept him as a man than as a figment of my unconscious mind.

At first I asked questions which could be answered by single words, but we were both puzzled and curious about each other and soon began to need more extended communication. So connected sentences were written but this was slow and clumsy work and one evening, after a specially strenuous burst of writing, one of the ivory wheels broke off and the poor little planchette sat down on its side for good. Next morning I was sitting at my desk considering a letter I had just received. My pencil was in my hand and I was idly tapping the back of the envelope when I felt the pencil pulling away from me. I eased my hand and lifted the wrist and the pencil moved easily into writing. 'Hard luck on poor Mary' it wrote. This was a direct reference to the contents of the letter and proof to me that Scott could read my thought even when it was not directed to him. I was illogically surprised that he should be here so far from our usual place of working. Now I was to become aware of his presence at any time of day and in any environment. But the first moment when he seized my pencil was filled with delight. After those years of abortive effort here was the ideal method of communication for my purpose.

We began to compare notes and Scott told of the road accident in which he had been killed. He has told the story of his death and 'translation' in another book* so it is not necessary to repeat it here. My pencil wrote on covering page after page as Scott continued the account of his existence since that last glimpse of a grey road had been shattered into oblivion. In time we came to his account of the seance at which he had first made contact with me. He was still in a condition where earth influences could reach him. He said:

'I had quite decided that these influences by which I was assailed were emanations of personalities from the world I had left. I followed one such trail until it became mixed with other and alien impressions. Then, startlingly, I began to 'hear' thought, a kind of running commentary, spasmodic, but easy to follow. Words like this came to me: "Now, perhaps ... The next? ... No. Almost the last at this rate. I wish I could see the tray better. Now, surely? No. Well, patience. Queer she is with her dreadful accent but a dear, kind soul I think. That's remarkable. Whatever can there be in those things to give her clues to their owner's character? Will she spot that what I have given her was Andrew's? What a weird business. Now ... Mine at last''. Following this came a queer, excited medley of thought. I judged this to be a woman's mind and she was listening intently to a voice whose words were blown through her consciousness to me in a strange echo. Then,

* *Post Mortem Journal.* Published by C.W. Daniel

36

undertow to this, I began to catch another current. It told me the conditions of the scene that was passing. This was a seance and there were a handful of people sitting in a dull little room. She gave me this picture in her thought, an uneasy undercurrent of sense of her surroundings. I saw my opportunity if only I could force my thought on the medium.

'With all my might I willed myself into her mind, tried hard to give her a mental picture of myself and implored her to speak of me. Can you place all this? Do you remember the "Egyptian" who offered to guide and help you? This was the fantastic guise in which the medium dressed me and not my doing at all though, funnily enough, there was a foundation in my past history for the thought of the white robe. Her description of my face amused me as she told you, but the whole thing was distorted by her notion of Egyptian local colouring. Hieroglyphics, indeed! What I tried to convey was my willingness to help you to understand, because I could feel that intense desire for knowledge straining through all your thought. So I followed you in spite of your amused disclaimer, determined to get through to your consciousness. Once I could pierce through your unawareness, get you to follow my thought, perhaps I should be able to transmit some reasoned proof of survival, my own at any rate. But it was not so easy. I was often non-plussed. After leaving that seance your thought faded out and I had difficulty in finding you again. I began to see how this thing worked. In times of excitement or heightened being you glowed into clear view and your thought came strongly to me. Then, not only was your conscious thought lit up for me, but also the deeper currents of your mind. Repressed and dangerous tides of sorrow, doubt and anxiety were painfully clear to me at times and were echoed by the vexed turmoil of my own inner self. I truly longed to help you and I lost no time in working on the nebulous currents that set towards me from your mind. I impressed your thought to keep you constant to your purpose and to find some means of communication. How you angered me at times! So near you would get and then the essential would get lost, but at last my chance came.

'I had realised that since your thought reached me, mine must reach you even though you were unaware of its source. Thought ruled body so why should not my strongly directed thought affect your control of your body? You gave me the chance to try this out when you began fooling about with that planchette. I despaired of moving a physical object which was invisible to me but I tried to direct its movements, nevertheless. To the confusion of theory it worked. My thought seemed able to move that clumsy contrivance though I failed to understand how. But it worked, thank God, and as soon as I realised your scheme of a circular alphabet I began to will the movements of the planchette. Remember that I couldn't see those letters except as a dim reflection in your thought and then you made it almost impossible by conscientiously refusing to look at them lest you had any hand in directing the thing. But I got my initials through and by a series of lucky hits I repeated them and at last arrested your attention. I sweated over the strain of making you take them seriously. But can you imagine my disgust when an easier way occurred to me? Of course if I could push the thing in one direction, by an extra effort of will I could surely make it form letters. The rest you know. With a great effort I pushed the pencil into forming letters and wrote my name. That was a moment of triumph the joy of which we shared. The next development was inevitable. I had grown very tired of pushing that clumsy toy when at last it collapsed. The notion that it would be far easier to push a human hand came next. You know, your startled laugh when I wrote on your envelope was lovely. Speed soon came and for me, ease of working. I have only to *think* my writing, not do it myself. I do it in thought and your hand automatically reproduces what I should have written in actuality. The style differs from your own, taking on something of mine, as one would expect. There is no magic nor nonsense about it; it is sheer thought transmission.'

Scott's writing ceased. There were several questions about this process. My chief fear had been that some trickery of the unconscious mind might produce a false response of its own which I should be unable to discriminate from an authentic one. As soon as my pencil began to move more freely I was disconcerted to find that I was sometimes aware in advance of the words to follow, anticipating the salient word or phrase as one does in recording one's own thought. Certainly an odd turn of phrase or an unfamiliar word would occasionally reassure me but I still felt strong doubts. Scott followed this thought and answered it.

'Let us understand the process better. I am near to you but not touching your hand nor attempting to push a pencil I can neither see nor feel. I just assume that it is in your hand and I picture the blank sheet of paper and the pencil travelling over it. Then I write mentally; that is, I do all that is involved in writing in imagination and your mind follows my thought-track. It moves your hand just as I think the operation. What does it feel like to you?' I reminded him how my pencil had pulled away from my control on that first occasion. It appeared to move entirely of its own volition. I did not will it to write his words and however hard I tried I was sure that I could not deliberately produce his writing. If I did try, it would be a slow and

39

clumsy counterfeit, whereas actually the poised pencil raced easily into his script. I could not even do my own familiar writing with any ease with my wrists lifted and pencil only poised over the paper. But doubts still lingered and Scott went on:

'I think the words on to your paper and that thought must be faithfully imposed on your brain which as faithfully guides your hand to its performance. Yet although some part of your brain must be the intermediary, your will is not involved and you are not originating the thought. Hence the feeling of automatism. Naturally you register also the advance thinking that one always has when writing, since my thought must go in advance of the effort to think words on to your paper. It is as though I transfer the will to motorise centres in your brain which then result in actions which produce writing of the same type as my own.'

That cleared up the process but how was it that Scott's thought could be so easily impressed on my brain? I took alarm at this and wondered if it was wise to allow such control to continue. Might it not gradually sap and weaken my will? My thought could not be hidden and Scott pounced on it at once.

'You forget that in the beginning it was your thought that was impressed on my brain. It is a mutual process so we are in equal danger of having our wills sapped and weakened. It is really nonsense to be so nervous. We are simply demonstrating the power of thought over body which belongs of right to my present state and that you are anticipating.'

This seemed to me a risky mixture of telepathy and hypnosis but experimenters must take chances. I privately resolved to hold my own. Forgetting that my thought could be read, I sensed a wicked chuckle from Scott. I caught the contagion of his laugh and it relieved the tension of my doubting mind.

Meanwhile, I continued to try in every way I knew to make contact with Andrew, my husband. I had told Scott about Andrew's message and he thought it was likely to be genuine.

'You have to remember,' he said, 'that he has been in this new world a long time and has friends and occupations that fill his time. You had his message some time ago and he may well have despaired of response. I expect he is trying again at intervals and we must be on the lookout to take any message that comes.' So I persevered.

By sitting quietly and gathering oneself for the effort it was possible to lift one's thought, to feel it reaching up and searching in higher levels of awareness. I found a useful mental picture was of myself standing outside a closed door in the dark, knowing that the door would surely open, although it could only be opened from within. I concentrated all my desire on trying to reach Andrew behind that closed door. Practising this technique one day I was certain of the impulse to write. I took pencil and paper and to my breathless joy my pencil began to form the well-known writing. To measure what this meant to me one has to realise what had gone before. During the early part of the war—1914–1916—Andrew's letters had been the crisis and meaning of each day and then had come the long weary years when I looked for them in vain although in dreams I was tantalised often by finding the thin envelope on the mat. Andrew had been posted as missing in 1916 and failing to get any confirmation of his death there had been the cruel years of hope deferred and its final extinction when the war ended. So now, twenty years later I saw again the long despaired of writing; no vaguely similar style, but the very same. It was not to be distinguished from that of his old letters when I put them side by side. The impact of his presence was great and our mingled joy and sorrow, wonder and love flooded powerfully into consciousness. We had a gulf of twenty years to bridge and for weeks we were busy linking up our so-different experiences. Andrew could read my thought and so was able quickly to scan its records, but I had to depend on the slower method of automatic writing to learn of his life and doings.

It seemed that he had found the work for which his ardent nature and quick sympathies best fitted him and had trained as a doctor to work among those ill-adjusted and emotionally sick people who so badly needed help in their new conditions. He helped me too, in what was for me a difficult time of re-adjustment and I gradually learned to take my experiences more calmly. He soon became interested in the effort Scott and I had been making towards an understanding of the relations existing between his world and this earth life. He brought to our enquiry his special knowledge of the make-up of the emotional body and his knowledge and influence will be apparent in all that follows.

As we worked at our theories we frequently had to admit ourselves beaten by insoluble problems. As though the concentration of our thought had reached another, we presently became aware that help was coming to us from another source. This unknown began to take a share in our discussions, breaking in with his characteristic writing when we were at a loss and sometimes over-ruling with benign wisdom our previous too-hasty conclusions. As we grew to know this fourth member of our group we found him to have a mystic's habit of thought along with serene

42

and patient wisdom. He told me afterwards that he had got on to the track of our thought because I sometimes read Carpenter's *Towards Democracy*, which was known and loved by him. So he had first been attracted by the current of familiar thought so unconsciously sent out by me. We owe him a great debt. His loving and wise friendship has been freely given to us and he has never ceased to inspire and guide us.

It took me some time to realise that my three friends were not within bodily reach of each other although they were able to communicate with me simultaneously. They were at different stages of development and therefore lived in different planes. Our new friend lived in more advanced conditions, Andrew was near enough to the lower spheres to work among those who had just reached them and Scott teased me by refusing to place himself at all. But the free interchange of thought went on through the medium of my pen and the reaction of mind on mind was clearly felt. This then, is the little group whose collaboration is responsible for what follows. E.K., our wise old friend is content to be known by his initials; 'Scott', who at this time withheld his real name because of his hatred of notoriety; my husband, Andrew. The script given by each of my communicators differs and is easily recognisable.

Scott writes thus:

To understand life study death.

E.K. has a pointed, sloping script:

And Andrew's neat writing is like this:

Undoubtedly my own style modifies the writing slightly but in the case of the only one I can compare with its earth counterpart, that of Andrew, there is little difference. The fact that I hold the pen lightly poised with the point just touching the paper and wrist raised makes it almost impossible for me to exert any muscular control.

Chapter Three

It was not enough to talk with my three friends, to take their writing and to learn all they could teach me about the life they were leading. The reality of their presence was a matter of experience to me but it had to be understood and stated in such a way that its truth linked up with the scientific truths all men accepted. I wanted to replace a vague hope of possible survival after death by a logical probability based on the nature of life itself; to push the confines of faith back, if ever so slightly and to enlarge the region of knowledge. To do this, I needed to pursue our knowledge up to the place where it thins out into a cloud of conjecture and then to collect from the other side of the cloud all that my friends could tell me of the nature of life as they knew it. Earth knowledge ends on this side in a mist of uncertainties, and beyond emerges that other knowledge which can never be generally acceptable until its connection with what is known and proved on earth can be traced clearly.

Contemporary thought seemed to my friends to be moving in a helpful direction. Atoms, once thought of as the ultimate units of matter had been resolved into smaller entities. The picture in men's minds of this world of the infinitely little had at first been of multitudes of tiny hard pellets held together by a law of attraction and revolving at great speeds in minute solar systems. But this simple view of matter had been superseded. Now matter, hard pellets and all had disappeared and in its place was energy; an electromagnetic field of force thickening rapidly in some regions of space and thinning out in others. The places where this field was dense our senses interpreted as solid matter, but actually it was a form of intense activity and its apparent solidity was entirely due to the speed of its vibrations. When a wheel is at rest one can pass a stick through its spokes, but set it whirling rapidly enough and any impact with the spokes will give an impression of impenetrability. So with the rapidly vibrating energy-packets which make up the atom. They are solid only because of their intense activity. All this is hopeful, because if matter can be thought of as a form of activity then the difference between the matter or activity we know on earth and that of which my friends' invisible bodies were composed became only a difference of degree and there was some hope of linking it up with our kind of matter, or activity.

So we come to the greatest puzzle of all—the organism, the living thing. How is the area of activity which is a living body different from any other area which constitutes dead matter? Chemically, it appears to be the same, yet it only obeys strictly chemical laws when it is dead. Then indeed, it makes haste to disintegrate and to re-enter the body of inanimate matter. Living matter and dead matter —both are areas of activity in the universal field of force yet the living patch of energy builds upon itself a variety of other activities ranging from independent movement, absorption of food, reproduction of its kind and so on to the highest energies of emotion and thought in the human being.

This range of additional powers must surely be proof of a profound difference between the two forms of activity. Yet in a moment of time all these extraordinary powers of the living body can be lost; death strikes the midnight hour which changes the princess back into the beggar maid. The area of dense activity which is the body suddenly loses all of its special powers and reverts to the merely chemical range of processes by means of which it is quickly reduced to the dust. That moment of death when, in the twinkling of an eye all is changed, surely holds the clue to the nature of what we call 'life'. What has happened to this particular patch of matter that it is so suddenly nothing *but* matter?

In the world of physical law nothing is ever lost. When an activity disappears in one form it must be sought in another. Thus, energy producing friction reappears as heat or light. The sum always adds up correctly and nothing is lost. We ought to be able to apply this same process to the body if those scientists are right who believe that living things are simply complicated machines formed of ordinary chemical constituents. Let us confront the scientist with a man at the point of death. The man moves, speaks to those about him, gives directions for his will, responds to the love and sorrow of his friends. Then the hour is struck and on the bed lies the very same assemblage of atoms arranged in just the same manner. How does he account for all the activities that are lost? His faith is that no energy is ever lost; he must therefore, acquiesce in his failure to account for the loss of all that made the thing on the bed a man.

If we say, 'Death is the end', what has science to do with ends? Its very existence depends on the faith that nothing ends but that everything changes and continues in a different form. Not a single scientific equation could be framed without assuming that nothing is lost. Let the scientific-materialist ponder the fact of death until he is moved to go in search of what he has lost—the whole range of powers and energies that make up a living personality. Thus I posed the question to myself, but who could answer it?

*　　*　　*

47

Scott worked perseveringly with me in the effort to relate his surviving self to the body he had left behind. I became conscious of his presence and now his writing replaced mine on the page.

'Let us look the exact facts in the face and see what they can be made to tell us. I once inhabited a body which for many years carried out a variety of activities. It studied, experimented, reached out for knowledge in all directions. It excavated in the east, explored and adventured in many parts of the world, played a risky and exciting part in war and in spite of wounds and misadventures was still intact and pretty useful to me. Somehow dependent on that body and bound up with it, I thought, to live or die, was a mind, a personality, emotions and thoughts which I would have sworn could not exist without it. Then what happened? A terrific jolt was given to the whole system by a quarrel with the law of gravity. Result: on a certain hard road was strewn the wreckage of two machines, one a thing of metal tubes and cylinders and one of chemicals in organic formation. But all the activities that had been associated with that smashed body of mine had vanished as far as any observer on earth could tell; that is, *I* had vanished. 'Well, here I am, well and active and that used-up machine of my body must by now be well on its way to dust. I say good luck to science if it is going to make any effort to trace those lost activities of mine. I shall do my best to give it some evidence of my continued existence.'

'I wonder why some people are so anxious to prove that death is the end?' I said. 'They will go to any lengths to show that survival is impossible and faith in it simply wishful thinking.'

'I also have sinned, don't forget,' said Scott. 'Perhaps psychology can help us to understand this tendency. It is

48

surely a kind of masochism, a stoic resolve to punish the wishful thinking one suspects is behind any belief in immortality. It feels very stern, strong and noble to deny the thing one secretly longs for, and so to prove that one is quite able to do without it. It is easy to find arguments to support this denial and see how superior it makes one feel to say "I, at least, do not need to believe in such things".

'But let us go on examining the facts as we know them. I have here the things which escaped from my body. Taking the crudest first, there is life, just the sheer power of feeling, moving and being in a body; then there is emotion—desires and purposes, to drive the body on its various occasions; then thought, the power to understand, to reflect, to plan, to reason; and lastly, there is a mysterious co-ordination of all these activities which is I myself, a personality which can look on at all these other activities and approve or criticise them. I give you that wretched body because I have most of the other things here and they are still in bodily form. Remember what was lost from earth-life, emotion, thought and the ego itself. These were all in the body of escape which detached itself from my injured physical body. There it was, and here it is; though I would thank anyone who could explain to me what 'here' and 'there' mean in this context. Space is another of those delusions which obstruct our thinking. If we could stop believing in space I think we might solve this problem more easily. But that is off the point. Go back now to my abandoned body. Apparently it has all the chemical elements within it as before, yet they all begin to function differently. The only possible inference is surely that from each of the atoms forming my erstwhile body something has escaped.'

'Wait a moment,' I said. 'Do you know that Professor

Whitehead asserts that an organic atom differs from an inorganic and that an electron inside the living body is different from one outside it?'

'He might have realised,' Scott rejoined, 'that the very same atom or electron must immediately *change* its mode of being when the organism dies and that in the twinkling of an eye something drastic has happened to it which sets it obeying different laws. That is the significant moment and it is at that point we have to account for the change which undoubtedly takes place. Here is what I think accounts for it: the organic atom is not so simple as the inorganic. By an increase of complexity it has produced a higher kind of atomic activity which is added to the normal rate of the atom. Keep well in mind the fact that the physical atom is also made up of activity but the new range of movement to which it has given rise becomes capable of an independent existence although this new atomic system, being in a higher range of vibrations, cannot be detected by sense or instruments. When the body dies this new range of activity is jolted free of the physical and forms the new body of which I, for instance, am composed.'

'Then life,' I said, 'is not some mysterious spiritual essence which leaves the body at death?'

'No. What leaves the body is the facsimile of the familiar earth body, built up atom upon atom on that body, but functioning in a different world of movement; at a more rapid rate, if you like, or in another dimension of being. What death does is to set this body free from its dependence on physical atoms, molecules and cells so that it can lift into an invisible form of activity. Do you follow?'

'I think so,' I replied. 'It would be true to say, then, that this other kind of activity mixed up with the physical

50

atom is what makes the difference between the two forms of matter, dead and living?'

'Yes, and when the higher activity is removed the physical naturally reverts to the inorganic kind of behaviour and instead of renewal and growth you get decay and disintegration.'

'Meanwhile,' I said, 'you who have become free of your earth body go your independent way in a very similar kind of body which yet is invisible to us?'

'An exactly similar body at first, as far as appearance goes, but there are striking differences in its powers and make-up which we ought to get Andrew to help us discuss. What I want you to realise is that the body I now use was being built up during my earth life and was always there interpenetrating my earthly body. It was the part of me that felt, desired, reasoned and thought but because it was based on the physical it was modified by that association. Thus I and many others were misled into thinking that these activities of feeling, desiring and thinking were *caused* by the physical. I know now that when I felt an emotion it was originated by what is my present body, even though it had the effect on my physical body of making my heart beat faster, or my brain to work in a certain way. These were effects, not causes, otherwise my present body would no longer be capable of emotion. It certainly is; I am getting very impatient with this argument as you can probably feel, since the whole thing is self-evident to me and I like to forget that I should have denied it all myself only a short time ago.'

'Let's stop, then,' I said. 'I have many more questions to ask you, but I am nearly choked with your impatience.'

'Sorry. It's harder to control feelings now than it was in the flesh. They were dulled by the drag of the physical, I suppose, and now they very easily get out of hand.

I'm going. It's too bad to make you uncomfortable.'

The 'Scott' consciousness, with its keen vision, critical regard and powerful emotions, faded out and I turned to other matters. The contrast between my ordinary self and that same self when re-inforced by Scott was remarkable. When he came, it was as though a narrow, petty stream of being had suddenly run into a broad and swiftly flowing river which carried on its waters in a stronger current. When his presence faded I always had some difficulty in reverting to my natural speed and habit of thought. On this occasion I sat quietly thinking over what had been said and trying to sum up the argument.

In the living body each material atom must be inter-penetrated by matter of another degree of being; as though the already swift system of movement had given rise to a still swifter vibration which was therefore lifted out of range of sight and feeling. Perhaps this invisible form of matter has many degrees since it has to carry activities of many kinds, some of a very subtle nature. Then living matter can be thought of as an ascending scale, of which only the lower and coarser notes are within reach of our senses or our finest instruments. All the higher notes, because of their finer vibrations thus make music which can never be heard by our ears.

How did these overtones come into existence? Directly they are present matter begins to show the qualities we associate with 'life'. A gradual process of development in matter itself, due to some uniquely favourable condition of the prehistoric ocean? However it occurred, life makes its appearance looking remarkably like an outcome of matter. Let us be content for the moment so to regard it. If living matter did indeed develop from non-living, it is under-standable that it remains bound up with the non-living and can only show its presence by moving and modifying it.

Similarly, it is natural that its absence should be proved by the cessation of movement and modification when the organism dies. Neither our senses nor our most delicate instruments can as yet trace the energies which have escaped, yet in each of us there exists this higher body which is our real being. Scott once said to me: 'Theorising will become unnecessary when the majority of mankind become able to register our presence, and when it becomes an actual experience to see us and feel us we shall have to be accepted as facts, even if we cannot be fitted into a theory. The trouble is that, lacking the experience, no theory, however plausible, is really convincing.'

So until such powers are generally developed we must continue to look for a sign. If life can be proved to be built upon the material atom known to science and to be just an extension of matter and subject to laws as ordered and unalterable as those which control the energies within the atom, then the mystery begins to clear. The great contribution of science to human thought is the faith that reality is a seamless garment and that all its manifestations are equally under the law. The apparently irrational is only the not-as-yet understood and where we cannot trace the operation of order it is likely that our vision of the facts is at fault. Surely, then, there must be some fundamental error in our vision of the strange thing we call 'life'. Perhaps we are too prone to think of it as a mysterious spiritual essence, something vague, formless and forever beyond our ken; whereas, if faith in the rule of universal order was stronger we might understand it clearly as the working *within* matter of the next degree of matter. Thus, when wounded tissues renew themselves, it is because the invisible body remains whole and the injured tissue is renewed in accordance with it. Growth then, must be the building up of the visible in correspondence with the invisible and the decay of the body in old age as the gradual drawing away of the invisible body as it gently severs its links with the physical order.

I had got thus far when E.K. made his presence felt and my pen began to record his pointed, sloping script.

'The probability is,' he wrote, 'that life is no mysterious supernatural affair, but *the most enduring aspect of matter*. You can injure or destroy the physical form but you cannot destroy the invisible body which interpenetrates it. Like any form of energy, life changes its form and thus escapes your detection, but no power in earth or heaven can destroy it nor prevent its continuance in form after form. For once matter, itself a form of energy, has produced this higher phase of activity, a new thing has been created which is beyond harm from your plane. It has entered upon an eternity of change and transformation and will go on to recur and develop until the end of time. So life, the delicate, the vulnerable, which appears to be at the mercy of senseless accident or malicious force— this tender thing when seen in its true character, is more enduring than the rocks and less to be defeated or confined than the ocean. It has achieved immortality having raised itself into a state of implacable continuance.'

We paused.

If I had sought to invoke necessity I had called it up now in an awful form. 'Implacable continuance,' I thought. What an awe inspiring phrase! No escape from life once life is achieved. We desire to be immortal and do not realise that there is no escape from immortality. Yet, if one once admits a process that raises dead matter to living matter one cannot stop the process there. There is always an immortality of causes producing an immortality of effects which in turn become causes. Thus the transformation of energy which has produced life cannot be reversed. It is a one-way progression.

This reminded me of what I had been reading about entropy. All lifeless systems of energy have a tendency to run down into a state of equipoise where no further interchange of energy is possible, just as things of different temperature give or take heat until they reach an equal temperature. It is inferred from this that the whole universe is running down like a clock wound up to go for only a certain time. When the state of equipoise, or entropy is reached the earth will be still and dead. Here again is a one-way progression.

Running counter to this is the process which our friend had described as 'implacable continuance'. Once life has been born of matter it must continue to take the upward trend into higher forms of energy, while lifeless matter pursues its hopeless way downwards towards entropy. This speculation began to be interesting for obviously at the point where life enters matter the two counter processes are engaged in the same entity. The organism is the history of their dual operation. The organism 'dies' when the life system draws away into continuance and the lifeless into disintegration.

E.K. broke into my reverie here:

'You took my thought well. Let me put it into my own words now. Two systems of energy are interlocked in the organism as you know it. They work together and modify each other and the whole story of the organism is the story of their gradual disentangling. They finally draw away from each other at death. The inorganic body is returned into the downward trend towards entropy and the invisible body of life is set free into the upward trend towards development. Of necessity it goes on to develop higher phases of activity for you must think of this body which is

55

only invisible to you, as being perfectly material on its own plane. Get rid of the notion of the ephemeral stuff of which phantoms are made. Life is simply matter which has been pushed upward into a higher phase of activity and has thus gained the power to exist and continue in another degree of being.'

'Then we need not despair if the universe *is* a doomed system which must inevitably run down into the silence of universal death,' I said.

'Not if you assume that all life will be drawn off the earth and capable of continuing without a physical form before that distant day arrives,' said E.K. 'But there are weighty and rather terrible considerations to be taken into account there. We will go into that more fully when you understand the necessity of rebirth. But now let us sum up the present argument.

'We assume one thing only: that energy is indestructible. We point out the failure of science to trace the energies apparently lost at death or to define the difference between the state of a "living" and "dead" assemblage of atoms. We conclude that a material atom is a patch of dense activity in the universal electro-magnetic field and that an organic atom resembles it but has created a further area of still more intense activity which interpenetrates the physical atom. This higher form of energy is invisible and intangible to you because it has lifted into a higher scale of frequencies. It is self-existent and draws off from the physical body at death in exactly the same form as the body it leaves behind. All the activities of life such as emotion and thought take place in this invisible body and are only reflected in the physical. Hence these powers which constitute the personality survive the separation from the physical.

'All living energy systems tend towards greater complexity and the consequent creation of higher forms of activity; all dead systems of activity tend towards greater simplicity and end in stagnation. The organism represents the interaction of both these processes and at its death they draw apart.'

With this masterly summing up E.K. ceased and we did no more that day. I knew that he was delighted to have got his thought through so clearly for a wave of keen pleasure swept through me as he finished. I was daily learning how real this interchange of emotions is and what a wonderful thing life must be when it is lived in this kind.

Chapter Four

It was interesting to theorise about the death-change but one wanted to know more. What does it *feel* like to leave the familiar body and the world of sense behind and to venture out into the unknown? What is this tremendous adventure likely to mean in terms of real experience? I had read accounts given to mediums which were substantially in agreement but Scott warned me here:

'I think the experience of death must vary considerably because it is governed by the state of mind in which one passes over. Also, there is a vast difference between a sudden passing and a quiet and prepared one. The shock of an unnatural death sets the invisible being in a mad turmoil and makes adjustment to a new environment impossible for a while. One finds oneself in a fantastic dream world with no continuity of experience. Flashes of vivid awareness burn themselves out into unconsciousness and the chaos of unconnected states of mind have no proper framework of space and time.

'Out of the sleep of death there comes first a mere sense of identity, a point of self-awareness growing out of nothingness. From this I judge that the higher activity of the ego-being is the first to assert itself. One wakes next to a tumult of emotions and hurried, anxious thought. Somewhere in this part of the experience comes the unrolling of memories. Your mind helps me to find a simile; it is like a speeded-up run through of a film shown backwards, a swiftly moving vision of life from end to beginning, flickering rapidly past the mind's eye until it ends in the unconsciousness of one's beginning. More unconsciousness follows and in my case the rest was a phantasmagoria. Glimpses of a world seen, clutched at and blotted out, dreamlike awareness of people and events on earth at which one grasped because of their dear familiarity only to realise that one could not make one's presence known. In the effort to do so the scene would melt and change into another. Then the final fading of earth and a long sojourn in what I think of as Hades, the place of the shade, a dim and formless world which I believe is peopled by the miasma of earth emotions and the unconscious projections of its inhabitants. Finally comes the stabilisation of the new body and a growing awareness of a real world again; light, clear outlines and real people moving about in a glorious world.

'Much of this earlier nightmare could have been avoided if I had known how to avail myself of the help that was freely offered. But I suppose the adjustment could not have been easy for me. I took over a very difficult make-up full of powerful repressions and tangled complexes all of which caused me much suffering before they were straightened out. My own obstinacy and pride were largely to blame for my plight. This was purgatory, if you like, but unavoidable unless one has done the job beforehand. I think I really had the maximum difficulties: an attitude of blank unbelief in any future life, a repressed and powerful emotional state, and the shock of a violent death. So this was not the normal passing but just a difficult and painful personal experience. I am satisfied that it was a just necessity and that I had made it inevitable by my wilful ignorance and scepticism. "Whatsoever a man sows" you know.'

I did know. I had experienced the overwhelming release of a long repressed grief and knew something of the dreadful power of such emotions. Purgatory, indeed. I knew something, too, of the resolute courage with which he had fought his way out of this nightmare. 'How do you account for these difficult experiences in terms of our theory?' I asked.

'I think,' said Scott, 'that the physical substance must act as a drag upon the new body rhythms and that where death is sudden and violent the new substance cannot at first free itself from the old physical rate. It yaws between the two and reharmonisation takes time. Probably periods of unconsciousness are the natural ways of bringing this about. In my case every kind of partial consciousness must have been experienced and you can imagine the weary confusion of it. Most of the time my senses didn't function at all and often I must have dropped back into the earth vibrations because I was aware of my friends and longing to make them realise my presence. When I tried to think a swiftly racing flood of images tore through my mind but they were incoherent and unmanageable. I could not learn how to control my emotions which were like an unruly army released from all discipline. But gradually this delirious confusion passed and my new body adjusted itself. My senses began to give me real knowledge of the world I had henceforth to live in.'

Scott's experience had indeed been stormy and chaotic, but fortunately E.K. could give a more reassuring account of the transition. He said:

'The normal experience is neither unhappy nor difficult. As old age comes on the two forms of being represented in the body begin to draw apart. Failing health and failing senses are the symptoms of this withdrawal. The brain tissues often seem to sever connections first before the other organs of the body are ready. This is the meaning of senile decay. When the final breath is drawn the process of

60

severance is practically complete and is rounded off by unconsciousness. Where death comes gradually and naturally like this one wakes quietly in the new conditions after an interval of a few days. One is fully through, as we say, and although the newcomer has to be cared for and kept quiet until the new rhythms of his body are fully established, he soon becomes strong and vigorous and ready to begin his new life. The transition, like all natural processes, should not be interfered with by violence or haste. Death is a kind of birth and it should proceed with a quiet inevitableness and not be accompanied by pain or distress. Much of the apparent suffering of a death-bed is not consciously felt by the sufferer. His real life is already half retired from the mortal body and neither experiences nor records its pangs. Shakespeare is very near the literal facts when he speaks of "shuffling off this mortal coil". Comparison of various accounts of the death-change make it clear that there are at least two stages, separated by intervals of unconsciousness. Actual death is followed by a period of unconsciousness which lasts for some time; this gives way to a kind of awareness but not a consciousness of one's environment. The new senses have not yet begun to function so there is nothing, or at best a misty, unreal setting, fantastic and dreamlike. During this interval, the memory appears to be stimulated so that one lives through a resumé of the life-time just past. Then one sinks into a second period of unconsciousness which should give place to a full awakening in the new world. We might with justice speak of a first and second death because not only the physical body has to be shed but the next body also. Think of the whole man as being composed of four interpenetrating forms. The second of these is very near to the physical in substance and is very closely knit to it. It is the etheric or life-body and gives the power of sensory experience. It never leaves the

61

physical body even in sleep but at death it parts from the physical along with the astral and ego bodies. It is too closely related to the physical to allow the higher bodies to pass clearly into their proper sphere, so it also has to be shed and this is the second death. Normally, it takes three days to disengage from the rest of the being and it is this transition period of which we have been hearing.

'Times can only be given approximately. As you have gathered from Scott's narrative, there are wide variations both in the nature and duration of this experience. I take it that most of this time is spent in sleep in normal cases but I also underwent at this time the rapid survey of my earth life. The etheric substance is the main instrument of memory, especially in its more mechanical aspects and this rapid recollection may be due to its loosening and withdrawal. Above all, it is necessary to emphasise that there is nothing to fear in any of these experiences if they are taken in quietness and confidence.'

E.K.'s helpful communication ended here.

All that I had been told of the change encouraged me to replace the fear of death with a lively interest and curiosity. Even if one cannot fully accept the information given here it is important that the right impression should be in the mind so that, however disconcerting the actual adventure may be we shall know how to accept it quietly and happily. There are many hands held out to help us and to ensure that our passing may be easy and natural. Our part is to allow ourselves to be helped and to await the outcome with confidence.

'It would help, perhaps, if you would give me a short account of your own experience,' I said.

'Willingly,' said E.K. 'I found myself awake in the transition state of which we have spoken. I thought myself still weak and ill, but I arose from my rest feeling marvellously refreshed and happy and I wandered for awhile in the something-nothing surroundings of this queer world and was unable to make any sense of it. The brooding silence drugged me into unconsciousness for a long time, because when next I woke my body felt quite different, no longer frail and weak as I had supposed, but vigorous and ready for anything as though I had suddenly stepped back into youth. This delighted me although I was daunted by my condition. There was a feeling of expectation, of waiting for something to happen. I was wide awake, quietly comprehending my state and content to sink into myself. Thought turned inward and it moved at a surprising rate. It raced over the record of a long lifetime which it lit up with a searchlight that spared no blunders, sins or weaknesses, but impartially illumined it all, as one holds up an old, finished garment to the light and notes with dismay its rents and stains. This clear blaze of recollection showed me the honest shape and cut of the thing too. I reviewed it as though I had no longer a special responsibility for it but had to understand clearly in what it had failed and in what succeeded. I was saddened enough and humbled by what I saw, and then, with a sigh of acceptance I was able to turn to other thoughts.

'My whole religious outlook had to be re-thought in the light of this unexpected experience. Naturally one had pondered on the meaning of death. I, like all reasonable men, could not believe that the life that left the body could utterly perish out of the universe. Now it was clear that I was still intact as a person though my present state was equivocal. Should I quietly fade out of this "place of the shade" or was this only the prelude to some wonderful afterlife? Then I slept again and so bade fare-

63

well to that sad place, awaking next in the lovely air on a sunny hillside. The interlude became a misty phantasm and but for its thought-processes might have had no more actuality than a dream. How the change took place I do not know, nor whether I passed out of another outworn body and left it behind. I could almost have thought at first that I was back in the world again, so happily familiar it all looked to my eyes which were greedy for the light and loveliness. But at last my mind began to assert control. I could think again and before I could find the desire to move or explore the scene I had to try to produce some order in the crowd of impressions and memories I had brought with me. I was not a methodical thinker so I had no pressing intent to make all these things fit into a logical series of causes and effects. I waited and let them flow into accord.

'Above all, I was happy. The lovely import of our journey from cradle to grave and through the valley of the shadow to arrive naked and reborn into this larger life, sang its themes of life triumphant until I was in an ecstasy of love and worship of the whole of which I was a rejoicing part. "Joy cometh in the morning" carolled itself through my mind; it could never have been meant for earth, that phrase, but for the morning of this new world.

'It seemed a long while since people had played any part in my life. The sense of their presence had faded out of consciousness during a long illness and since its close I had been solitary. I had no desire to find companions and now my eyes were filled with beauty and I could think of nothing but its unearthly joy. As I lay there on the hillside I left behind all sorrowful musing and gave myself up to the sheer rapture of satisfied senses. This was no earthly beauty. There was a light *on* things and *in* them so that everything proclaimed itself vividly alive. Grass, trees and flowers were so lighted inwardly by their own beauty that the soul breathed in the miracle of perfection. I was utterly content. From all these glorious things there streamed a light of their own. Colour and fragrance were not a tincture of their substance as on earth but were the very life they shed forth upon the lovely air. The air itself had a light in it, a sense of being life in itself and as one breathed it the last choking fumes of earth were banished from the body's recollection. I thought of all the hackneyed similes we used on earth—air like wine—and so on, but here they were statements of fact. The air is wine, the light is life. The gleams of meaning which substance reflects on earth had become the actual being of things. One perceived them by way of their meaning and saw less by sight than by understanding.

'I am almost at a loss to describe the heavens as I saw them from my hillside. The light radiated from no one direction, it was a glowing, universal fact, bathing everything in its soft radiance so that the sharp shadows and dark edges which define objects on earth were missing. Each thing glowed or sparkled with its own light and was lighted as well by the circumambient splendour. The sky, as I looked upward was like a vast pearl gleaming with opalescent colours. There was a suggestion of unfathomable depths of space as the shimmering colours parted their transparencies to show the infinite abyss.

'I was awakened from my absorption by the sound of voices. If the loveliness of tree and flower had held me spellbound my first sight of fellow beings gave me more cause to rejoice. Here was another form of life, a more complex one which also emanated its own lovely qualities in visible rays. These people were more than alive; life streamed from them, palpitating with their emotions, lit and splendid with their joy and waxing and waning with its intensity. Here, again, bodies were not defined by shadows and the softer outlines were glorious with the outflowing life. I trembled at their approach and felt like an interloper from a lower sphere. They came towards me, greeted me and reassured me. I had been feeling like a strayed mortal in heaven until they came; now I had to realise that I was one of them and was glad to go with them and learn of them something of the conditions of my new life.

'I speedily grew used to my new form. My body has wonderful lightness and resilience and it is as though the thought and desire of motion can move it without any cumbersome machinery of muscular action. This more vital body, so pulsating with life is quick to respond to thought and emotion. Each passing phase of feeling glows and pulses through it visibly, irradiating it with colour and meaning. You have heard talk about the aura and with your habitual distrust of the fantastic have doubted. What I have been telling you is just a description of the aura. It is simply the outgoing life, the emission of life in the form of emotion, true always to its origin in the being. This self-revealing is unavoidable, automatic. Now are you a little more resigned to the thought of an aura?'

I was becoming used to this kind of gentle teasing.

'As an isolated phenomenon I was shy of it,' I replied. 'But now that you have shown me that all living things breathe out the life that is in them I am more satisfied. I can relate it to some transient impressions of living things that have sometimes startled me by their beauty.'

'Yes, it is present in all living things on earth as well as here. I could spend a long while telling of the rhythmic patterns of vibrating light and colour which can be seen here, but I know your instinct to keep your feet very firmly on the ground, so I will refrain. I suppose if I can

66

link this up with a theory about the emission of photons of energy in the form of light you may accept it, but that is not my way.'

A new kind of consciousness, a new quality of being should be reflected in better adjustments between individuals and hence all social values would be altered. Utopias are always doubtfully valid because their creators take with them into their promised land an unaltered humanity, so faith in the ideal order is impaired by one's knowledge of the insufficiency of human nature. But faith in a new order would be easier if there were fundamental differences in consciousness, and in the accounts my friends had given of such modifications there was justification for belief.

My first distrust of a too-easily won heaven had been dispersed by the accounts Scott and Andrew had given of the gradual process needed to straighten out the tangles in earth-disordered minds. Though it seemed strange that man should take pain with him into this far less physical kind of life, yet enough mental suffering was felt on earth to make this tenable. Now what of man as a gregarious animal? Did he still form religious communities and national groups? Here I had no expectations and I began to take our friend's next communication with great interest.

'To understand the social aspects of our life you will have to take into account certain factors you have not yet got into focus. Remember that these planes of being have been in existence as long as the advent of man and so have a long history. That appears to startle you but why should you suppose that they have been recently created or that they should not also have woven their own story? We have a legacy of history here as you have and naturally there has

67

always been a relatedness between the two orders of life. Earth events are very often the offspring of spiritual events and the world here is continually influenced by the happenings of earth. Conditions on earth tend to be reflected here as the protagonists of great movements come here. It is to be remembered that their great ideas have invariably had their origin in powerful movements of thought on these planes. So the interrelated web is woven between us, and on your side you write your one-sided histories and on this side we have our fuller records.

'Human souls have always spent far longer on these planes than on the earth itself; the tenure on each plane here has no set period. Those who develop quickly may pass on within a few years of their coming, others who mature more slowly may spend centuries here. So these planes of being are really to be thought of as the true home of the human race. The earth, in spite of its importance as a preliminary training for another great cycle of living, is a kind of exile. Here with us is the bulk of living experience both in numbers and time. On the next plane there are less people and as one goes up I believe that the numbers continue to decrease. At each stage a certain number return to earth as they attain to the final development of which they are capable.

'It would be fascinating to trace the parallel histories here and on earth. The comparison would be illuminating because the new factors in experience annul the greatness of some famous people and enhance that of others. All your historical characters have to pass through these planes and they add their typical quota to our history as they have done to yours. Where there has been true greatness of emotional being it makes itself felt again here and this is so whether the power is good or evil. But power exerted as evil destroys itself here. Its exercise is intolerable both to its wielder and to his world. The moral law is now set anew as a physical law and this makes the early years on this plane as chequered a story as on earth even though the grosser forms of violence are left behind. Where a man has power of an evil nature he spreads such suffering around him and will attract such suffering to himself that life will be intolerable to him. He will be abandoned by all and become an isolated misery until he comes to himself. He will have to work out the inner conflicts which are at the root of his anti-social tendencies and when they are resolved he will be sane and happy again.

'This law of suffering as the result of emotional disease is a great regulator of society. You know that fire burns and so avoid putting your hand into the fire. With just as much conviction we avoid anger because we know that it will burn us in just the same actual sense. That is the negative side of things; positively, a happy, loving man is the riches of the community.

'You are thinking now of some of the ghastly wrecks that must have come up here as the result of the grosser evils of the past. It must indeed have been so, but remember that here life itself is on our side. It is no longer fighting a losing battle against its physical manifestation. There is no death; life is bound to win. Of its own nature it is good and beautiful. As it becomes more abundant it aids the sufferer. He absorbs healing from his surroundings and he is relieved of pain as he takes in the rays of love and healthy life from those who tend him. The very life within him cries out against the deathly elements which are harming him and the goodness and potency of life free him gradually from the fever and pain of wrong living.

'Now for the next stage of our life here, which will please you less perhaps because it is less like earth and more like heaven. Nations keep their own languages and customs but they are less defined because movement has become more simple—not more simple to explain, as we shall find when I try to tell you what it is like—but more simple to effect. Thus there is much coming and going among us and our sympathies are wider and knowledge of each other fuller. The language barrier begins to be removed because it is so much easier to pass thought between us. Groups are formed more for the purposes of special interests and occupations than for national reasons and thus we get aggregates of talent of a high level of attainment which cut across all artificial boundaries of nation and class. Here are brotherhoods of mutual interests having a rich and satisfying communal life. Co-operative activity and close and sympathetic human relationships bring into being many of the ideals of the world's dreamers. A social order emerges which brings satisfaction to all its members and enables each to arrive at full self-development.

'We can be still more independent of elaborate details of living if we please, but what you call the "lush" side of life has adherents even here. Gleaming palaces and temples and beautiful cities built in elaborate form in surroundings of surpassing loveliness do exist. They satisfy the artistic and creative among us, so have a legitimate place in life after all. They cannot be anything but beautiful; they are too instinct with meaning. You may yet be sorry for your scorn of that kind of ornate life one day. Much of such gorgeousness remains to us from the past and is mellowed by age and association. I feel that I want to reconcile you to it, because in spite of my own preference for simple joys I cannot but be stirred by its beauty. Words of description are vain.

'The people suit their glorious home. They are noble, dignified, happy and fulfilled. They have the glow and splendour of a wonderful maturity. All the emotional disorders of the lower planes have been cured and so the full growth obstructed by them can come quickly to fruition. There is less specialisation in human relationships and no sense of possession in even the more intimate relationships. The possession of love in oneself implies that one is fully alive and healthy and it must flow freely out to mingle with the love it seeks and finds in others. Freedom has come to it at last and the barriers we set up on earth to protect our special rights of possession are no longer necessary. Life has come of age, you see, and so love can come of age also.

'We spoke before of the enlargement of consciousness and of the increasing scope of the "now". That development is taken a little further. The sequence of states of consciousness flows quietly by gathering still more of the future into the present. There is a lucid flow of being which alters one's sense of duration and adds beauty to the mere passing of time as it collects to itself the lovely future and passes it into the still lovely past.'

'How we must strain and tug at your even flow of thought,' I said, 'when you have to follow the jerky, inconsequential instant to instant progress of our minds.'

'Yes, you continually pull me up by questioning what is here when I am dwelling on the subsequent image. If you would be more docile and not attempt to criticise and appraise what you are writing word by word I could get through my thought in far more characteristic form.'

'I am distressed by the trouble I must cause you and still more sorry that I have increased it by lack of understanding,' I said. 'But please go on and I will practise docility.'

E.K. patiently complied.

'Just a word more about the people here. All material forms have thinned out and have more of light and colour

71

and less of delineation. Appearance has approached still closer to meaning. The two are often widely sundered on earth, but with each lift of being life makes a fresh conquest of its embodiment and constrains it more nearly to its own nature. Here the colour and shape of a flower is its own perfect presentment of its essential being. It shines out clearly in the form of light so that a shimmering radiance abides continually over field and woodland. Is the change wholly in our environment or partly in ourselves? Is this glory objectively real or is it that our eyes see more truly, so that with a more sensitive awareness we may possess more of the meaning and joy of all things? But that which has life has actual being in its own right and is not merely a chance collection of sense data presented for our interpretation. As we progress we see things more wholly in terms of their own essential being and less in terms of related patches of colour and delineated form. I lose myself in the effort to convey this to you and then find that you have an instinctive knowledge of it and are anticipating my description. Whenever I am happy in getting a true image to you there is that intimation of something immediately recognised and loved. It is the standard of comparison whereby you unconsciously test all that I give you. It is the deeply hidden memory which comes up into consciousness in the form of hunger for the beautiful and true.'

I was puzzled about the kind of matter which must constitute this new world. It had been permissible to try and trace the lost properties of the living being as they escape at death, because here in the organism are the properties of a non-material existence, but how could links be found between the matter of our earth and this other world which was completely hidden from our senses although in time and space I was told that it occupied the same region? In what way were the two degrees of matter related or did they exist in complete independence of each other? I knew from what my friends had told me that as we come and go on this earth we are literally moving through the space of the other world, traversing its scenery and jostling its inhabitants. Yet we remain entirely unconscious of their presence and, except in rare cases they cannot be aware of us. But they walk on solid earth as we do and their world is diversified with hills and valleys, rivers and seas and is clothed with trees and plants in abundant beauty. Can it be that all our matter has a dual aspect and that in its super-material being it exists in the after-death world? If this is so, the landscape there must be feature by feature a repetition of this earth of ours; city for city, hillside for hillside and tree for tree existing in a kind of enchanted being just across the boundaries of sense and vision. The notion was romantic enough. It reminded me of the magic transition into the 'land of faerie', the 'stepping across the fern' of Irish folk-lore. But practically I could see difficulties in the idea. It made the next world completely dependent upon what we chose to do in this one. If we pulled down a house, down it must come in both worlds and if we cut down a wood and built a city the wood would disappear and the city appear as by magic in the other world. The notion was obviously untenable and I had hardly finished smiling to myself at the ludicrous situations we might create for our friends there when E.K. came to my rescue.

He said:

'It is very difficult to see how the matter of this plane is connected with yours. You remember how often we have tried to relate your mere location with our space and have failed. You are here, we say, and then, no, you are gone and we find you away over a distance again. Even when you

73

make a long journey in your space you may not move far in ours and attempts to follow you, to travel with you, produce the most nonsensical results. Do you remember being set to walk out various angles of a figure taking a certain number of paces for each side? You were very puzzled and indeed a little cross that we required such unreasonable things of you. We were making a deliberate attempt to find some relation between movement in your space and in ours but we were not able to interpret the results. So you will realise how difficult it is to make any useful comparisons.

'There does seem to be a certain similarity in the nature of the landscape but not enough for us to think of actual super-position. Natural features are sometimes alike hill with hill, forest with forest but the disposition of water in our plane has not much relation with yours. While you are sitting quietly there, your position is for once stationary. Your present site* in our world is a wooded slope with a large tree close to your chair. That is a scene not unlike what must have been there before your present town was built, but it is odd to think that there is a tall tree growing right through the centre of your tall house in our space and that you are quite unconscious of it.

'It is perhaps significant that our cities appear to correspond with waste and lonely places on earth and that the sites of your busy cities are avoided by us and are waste and lonely in this world. Your speculation about the dual nature of matter will not do. If it were so, we should be interfering with each other all the time. But even though this is impossible I still have to insist that our planes interpenetrate the earth levels just as they interpenetrate each other and the problem of the independent material substance of each of these worlds within worlds is still

* House on the outskirts of a small town.

74

unsolved. What wonderful scope for your mathematicians!'

'But after all,' I said, 'our picture of actuality is rather an arbitrary one since it is nothing but the way in which our minds interpret our sense impressions. Surely other beings, with different sensory equipment and different mental make-up might get a totally different picture of actuality. If matter is only the denser areas of the electromagnetic field, there could be many possible ways of interpreting it. Is it not possible that your different world is simply due to your different make-up?'

'You mean that the actual patches of denser activity which you interpret as matter are the same for us but that we understand them differently and so produce for ourselves a different world?' E.K. replied. 'No, although that is a fascinating variation on your other suggestion, it will not do. To begin with we have agreed that your patches of dense activity, your matter, in fact, is non-existent for us since it is vibrating below the level of the frequencies which can be registered by our senses. Our matter must of necessity be based on vibratory systems which are within our field of activity and they are bound, therefore, to be beyond your scale of visibility. No, only your organic matter can have any reality for us. The etheric matter which is found in plants and animals and in your bodies is similar to the physical matter of our lower planes. There are many different grades of etheric substance and the human kind differs from that of the plant. Apart from any living organism on earth there is a great envelope of free etheric matter associated with the mass of the earth itself. All of these forms of etheric substance we may class as matter of the second degree only one remove up from your mineral matter. Our living, beautiful world is built up out of this second degree matter but if it has any links with the structure of your world they are most difficult to discover.'

'Then the whole range of our kind of matter is non-existent for you; even light waves, which have the highest frequency do not affect you at all?' I asked.

'Not as visible phenomena,' was the answer. 'It is considered here that your light affects our atmospheric pressure but it certainly does not register on our senses. No sun, moon or stars shine in our skies. Light pours down uniformly from all parts of the heavens and light, for us, has a necessary connection with life. For all living things here emit light of their own and as one goes higher, life is expressed still more in terms of light and less in substantial form. Almost unconsciously, we infer that the light which pours down on our world is a kind of life. It renews our being, and satisfies and feeds us; in fact, we need no other food. This light shines continuously and constantly renews our life in vigour and joy.'

'If you have no night, do you never feel the need for sleep?' I asked.

'No, rest perhaps, but not sleep. You only crave for sleep so that your astral and ego bodies may be set free for refreshment in our living air. They become exhausted by their interaction with the clumsy physical matter of your body and so must be released regularly into what is really their native atmosphere.'

'Then during sleep, does the super-physical body move away from the living, breathing thing on the bed?'

' "Move away" suggests a removal in your space and that is not ours. No; the astral and ego bodies are released from their dependence upon the physical and lift into harmony with this world perhaps without moving at all in terms of your space. It is a matter of being set free from their dependence upon earth rhythms. When you sleep the higher ranges of being which are as much a part of your body as what you politely call "the thing on the bed" are

76

able to lift clear into their own unhindered rhythms and so obtain relaxation.'

'But they have no real consciousness apart from the body,' I objected.

'Earth consciousness is the result of a close co-operation between all the forms of being represented in a man. Before the astral and ego bodies can achieve full consciousness by themselves they have to make the adjustment to new conditions we have discussed in connection with the death-change.* But we are wandering from the point. We set out to try to discover whether there are any links between our material world and yours. I have thought that the senses record and interpret differences in a kind of reality which is governed by the light which is our source of life. That needs more explanation. This life-giving light of ours has its own scale of frequencies which differ for each plane. That means that the senses of the inhabitants of the various planes are able to register that particular range of frequencies as light. Here I make a leap of faith and suggest to you that this living light is the thought and love of God made visible. I believe that it must stream down equally through all the planes whether it is visible or not. I think that we have here the great creative agency, which, while it illumines, also crystallises its meaning in the different degrees of space which we then interpret as patches of matter. These material forms have consequently for us something of the meaning and purpose of God to which their being is due. Light is a form of activity, very intense activity, the highest known to us on any plane. Therefore, it may well have the power to influence activity and even to create it.

'If this is indeed the creative power, we have in us a

* See *The Fourfold Vision*, published by Neville Spearman, for a full consideration of this subject.

similar form of being, since we also in our small way emit the light of the life that is in us. This enables us to read meaning into matter and in an imperfect way, no doubt, to interpret the mind of God in his works. The world of meaning is the world of reality; here we get nearest to the mind and purpose of the Creator. Matter in any plane is the manifestation of that meaning in terms of the activity which will bring it within range of our senses.'

'Not easy,' I said. 'But we certainly do not apprehend matter as patches of activity. We immediately make a creative act of our own and endue it with meaning. A sunset does not consist for us of vibrations with different wave-lengths, but of living colour, full of beauty and meaning. You think that we perform a kind of imitative creative act when we interpret matter which has some relation to the original creative act by which God calls it into being?'

'Yes,' said E.K., 'and this idea has the merit of being equally applicable to our worlds and to yours. We have the advantage only in the fact that the creative light is visible to us. I believe that it shines on earth as well but is unperceived by you. That is what I meant when I said the earth is a realm of spiritual night.'

'Let me try to piece together what you have told me,' I said. 'I have to envisage world within world, each peopled with beings with senses attuned to different ranges of vibrations in a universe of manifold activity. Each of these interpenetrating worlds is equally actual, since they are differing versions of the meaning of God. I have to think of the Creative Activity under the symbol of light, which is an intense form of activity crystallising into specific forms of meaning, which provide the material setting of the life of each plane. The basis of all matter is the thought of God directing activity and making it actual in every sphere.

Not so simple as I thought, but far more satisfying. So, as I sit here, if I had the developed vision, I could close my eyes to this room and sit under the great tree that grows in your world. Again, if I could clear my vision still further I might open my eyes upon a still more beautiful kind of reality and so on until I had explored my "real" surroundings in all possible worlds. But my inward sight is as yet blindness and only the walls of my room are actual to me. It is sad.'

Afterwards I remembered Francis Thompson's words:

> *When thy seeing blindeth thee...*
> *To what thy fellow mortals see;*
> *When their sight to thee is sightless;*
> *Their living, death; their light, most lightless;*
> *Search no more—*
> *Pass the gates of Luthany, tread the region Elenore.*

Chapter Five

In spite of these conclusions about the separation of the planes from each other, I suspect that man is never completely free from the influences that stream in even though he remains unconscious of them. Yet to establish deliberate contact means a long process of psychic development. It was clear from the previous discussion that the *matter* of the various planes was unrelated and that our solid-seeming earth was non-existent to the dwellers on other planes, as their material world had no actuality for us. This required an act of faith when the imagination was challenged to picture it; almost too much faith, I thought, if I had to make myself believe that all my substantial surroundings were so much thin air for a dweller in these planes and that his substantial surroundings were all about me yet not to be known by me. We were walking into and through each other's actualities all the time and could not know it. Cold doubt seized me.

True, I had become convinced of the reality of my friends, but I only knew of their presence by the strong inner feeling of their personalities which they conveyed to me. While they were with me I had no fear, but there were times when their friendly presences were far off and then cold waves of doubt assailed me. A shivering cloud of cold unreality dimmed the outlines of both worlds for the moment. As I struggled to emerge from it I became aware of the patient and serene presence of E.K. who so often bore with me and helped me clear of these miasmas of doubt. He ignored my faithlessness now and quietly went on to write for me. Confidence and tranquillity flowed back as the steady writing went on.

'You are forgetting,' said he, 'that the material structure of a man's body is other than the solid-seeming things which have suddenly smitten you with a true sense of their illusory nature. These things have no intrinsic reality. For you they are, and for us they are not. But there are elements in your body which *have* real being on our planes. Under exceptional circumstances men may become visible to us here. They "come through" temporarily, as at death they will come through finally, into this larger life. The visibility of a man's appearance here is largely dependent on the degree to which he has developed the substance in his being which belongs to our planes. The power to come through may be there in many men who refrain from using that part of their being and so they remain invisible beyond the earth sphere.'

'You think of that as a kind of spiritual stature?' I asked.

'Yes, a man's stature is important because to have real being on any one of our planes while still on earth is to be able to bring down its influence into the life of your world.'

'Yes, I see that would be so. You said that only organic matter had any real existence for you and also that etheric matter formed the material substance of your world. Help me, please, to understand to what extent the human body is visible in your sphere,' I said.

'In spite of the fact that you have etheric, astral and ego elements in your being, it is seldom that a dweller on earth becomes fully visible to us. It is as rare a happening as for you to see a ghost. Let me try to explain why this is so. The interlocking of your etheric and astral with the physical structure appears to obliterate your real being for us. It is all "timed down" to the physical, as Scott would say, and so shares in its invisibility. Only very

81

occasionally does your astral body glow through the darkness in which you exist. The ego-life is also invisible to us except in its effects on the astral, but the thought which is its form of activity travels freely in our spheres and there must always be an interchange of thought going on between us.

'I should warn you that there is an important distinction between thought as you understand it—a matter of working up by means of the intellect of ideas intuitively apprehended, and our form of thought which is far nearer direct intuitive knowledge than a logical process. Our thought can only reach you in the shape of an intuition of truth. You have often experienced this when a formless idea has reached you and your intellect has had to work hard to formulate it in words. Our side of the problem is in finding words in your mind to present the more fluid knowledge with which we deal. But to come back: it amounts to this. Any man on earth has real being on at least three planes. His physical body, rooted in the mineral structure of the earth itself is his visible body in your world. His etheric and astral bodies give him affinity with our planes and his ego-body links him with higher planes still. Of these forms, all but the darkness of the physical form can sometimes be seen by us in terms of light. The etheric is dim, but the astral gives a great variety of colour and light forms and is a certain index to character and development. The ego-life, though itself invisible is the creator and modifier of the pattern of the astral structure and thus makes a visible sign of its presence. So in most men on earth are represented the typical substances of the succeeding planes; thus in the human form one has all the links between the worlds.'

'The ego-principle, being formless even to your vision,

is nearest to the old idea of a spiritual body?' I said.

'Yes,' said E.K. 'What it is in itself we do not know because it only betrays its presence by its influence upon the other bodies, but certainly the appearance of this higher principle is what marks off man from the animals. The future development of the human race is probably indicated as the gradual penetration and control of all the other bodies by this ego-principle. Meanwhile, intuitive thought, the special ego activity is entirely free of the earth categories of time and space and so is the only activity that can pass unhindered between all planes of existence.

'In the case of the mystic, the poet and the sensitive, glimpses of our world may sometimes be caught, yet I suspect that the vision of the seer is often the reception of a thought form so vivid as to create in him all the effects of sight. You have not yet appreciated the quality of our sight. It is the power of *inward* seeing developed to such perfection that it takes the place of outward sight. Outward and inward sight work together for us so that when we see a thing with our outward eyes we see it even more keenly with the "eyes of the mind" as you would say; only that does not begin to express the keenness of understanding which accompanies the act of sight.'

'Are we beginning to use that power when we recall a memory picture?' I asked.

'No: it differs entirely from a memory picture. That is quite dead. It belonged to time and time has killed it. The vision I mean can be developed by you, but only at the cost of much meditation and patient endeavour. You have had rare glimpses of it and should not cease working for it.'

'I regard those few moments of illumination as the most wonderful experiences of my life,' I said. 'You know how much I value them. But I am slow to develop and the details of living are too demanding to give me the necessary leisure.'

'Remember the pearl of great price,' said E.K., 'and revise your scale of values. It is important to go on once you have started because it is dangerous to arrest a process of development once it has started.'

'One more question before you go,' I said. 'If a man has consciously tried to develop the powers of thinking and being in your spheres of activity, is it really a help to him after death?'

'We have spoken of the etheric, astral and ego-bodies,' said E.K., 'but you would be dismayed to realise how little developed the two latter forms can be even in a man of high moral and mental worth. When the average man lays by his physical form and his etheric body also melts away, very little is left to face a new life. His resulting form is often so tenuous that he needs a long period of rest and treatment before his new body is fit. The less he has trained and controlled his emotional nature the less formed will his astral body—now his *visible* body, be and the longer time he will need for preparation. His astral body, so poor, weak and unformed is now the only outward form he possesses and its condition depends entirely on the building up of his desires and emotions in his earth life. So frequently the emotional life has been either starved and neglected, or else allowed to become chaotic and diseased. It may even be deformed because of habitual indulgence in evil desires and feelings.

'These facts should be widely known and taken into serious consideration in order that a worthy astral form may be built up there. So much depends on the man's actual condition when he comes here. The state of his astral body judges him and decides the nature of his after-death experiences. One needs no worse hell than the torment of living in a diseased and suffering astral body.'

'I see. My question was a foolish one.'

'Not foolish,' said E.K., 'but an echo of an attitude too often met with on earth. I have often heard people say, "If I live a fairly decent life I don't see what more can be expected of me." That attitude is very mischievous. There is no easy road to heaven, as we were warned long ago. Where the work of purifying and developing the emotions is not done well on earth it has to be done here. The debt we owe to life is harder to pay then, and involves much weakness and suffering.'

'It is very deceptive, then, this flesh and blood body of ours,' I said. 'Queer to think that behind some of the imposing façades of dignified and imposing mortals is only a wraith-like tenant, sickly and feeble. It reminds me of the Shakespeare sonnet:

' "Poor soul, the centre of my sinful earth,
    Fooled by these rebel powers that thee array,
    Why dost thou pine within and suffer dearth
    Painting thy outward walls so costly gay?" '

Naturally, I puzzled often over the not-clearly-understood process by which my friends communicated with me. I appealed to Scott:

'I want to get quite clear about the process by which I think your thoughts and take your writing,' I said. 'Although our worlds are completely cut off from each other, there must be a link by means of which you are able to move the physical matter of my hand and to influence the thoughts that form in my brain. Can you make me understand how this comes about?'

'I will try,' said Scott. 'There are, as you know, the four principles of being represented in your make-up: physical, etheric, astral and ego. I share with you only the two last, so any influence I am able to exert on you must be by way of the astral or ego-being. Each of the four principles has its own characteristic form of activity; the physical generating force by means of chemical changes, etheric producing changes in the level of life-energy and releasing this in the form of living activities, astral energy working by fluctuations of emotions and thus releasing waves of feeling to be absorbed by the bodies of those around, and lastly, the mysterious ego-life, invisible and intangible, yet able to fling its messages into space-time with a speed which cannot be calculated and a range which is infinity.

'An emotion is generated in my astral body, shall we say. It may be directed specifically to you but, with or without my consent it will spread outwards from my body and affect anyone within a limited range. In my world it would be seen for what it is, good or bad, ugly or beautiful, since it will spread around me in its characteristic light and colouring. The pattern of its rays will also give indications of the kind of thought which accompanies it.'

'I cannot see a wave of emotion,' I said, 'but I feel it quite keenly, as you know. My sensation is not of something impinging on the surface of the body but of slow waves of a recognisable kind spreading through me, causing delight or pain according to their nature.'

'I am sometimes sorry that you cannot see the colour and form of my aura,' said Scott, 'since it would tell you more of my meaning than mere words, or the sensory impression you do get. But I admit that at other times when anger or impatience master me I am very glad to be invisible to you. But see what happens when you receive such a wave of emotion. It permeates your astral substance since it is an astral emission, but it has a reflected effect upon the etheric and physical substance and must reach your consciousness by way of the ego-being.'

'But I do not always understand the meaning of the

emotional wave until you have sent some kind of message to explain it,' I objected. 'Something may give me pain which shudders right through me into the physical body but I may not have a clue as to its source or meaning.'

'No: strange. I can sometimes by a deliberate effort keep my thoughts from you but the emotion that accompanies them inevitably reaches you. It looks as though thought can be better directed and controlled than emotion but even so it will reach you if it has affinity with your own thought, directed or not.'

'When you intentionally send thought to me I sometimes get it in a queer way,' I said. 'It is not a picture and it does not come in words. It is as though a shining ball is tossed to me. I know it is important and I have quietly to receive it and wait for it to unroll so that I can find words for it. I suspect that you also supply suitable words sometimes, because as I unwrap my ball, the words come so cleanly to hand. But the whole idea is first tossed to me instantaneously and the finding of words is a separate process.'

'But I don't supply the words myself. I only select from those I can find in your mind and this is why your limitations affect the giving of the message. It is very seldom that I can get you to use a word you do not know. With great difficulty I have sometimes made you spell out an unfamiliar word but your faith is not very strong and you usually hang back and make it very hard. So I usually have to be content to use the tools with which your mind provides me.'

'I'm afraid we have to accept that limitation,' I said. 'But can you explain this transmission more fully?'

'It is like this: I send a thought. You see that transmission of a whole idea or group of ideas as a shining ball tossed to you. Queer, that. It is probably an intense ray which may have the nature of light in some remote sphere but which is not so visible to me. If a ray with a very high frequency suddenly shoots into your slow space-time continuum might it lose its character of a ray and appear to your mind as a ball? I wonder. It might be interesting to follow up that idea, but never mind it now. However it comes it must be received by your ego-being which it must modify. The modifications then spread through the rest of your make-up and when they reach the etheric-physical brain a reflecting process takes place which mirrors them back into consciousness. Then you decode the message and fit words to it out of your store and so the thought I sent is finally expressed in your terms.'

'Hmm; thank you. That is when I get the thought and have to find my own words. But what about this writing?'

'That's easier,' said Scott. 'When you become receptive to me I can think I am you and use your body as though it were my own. My thought and intention would move my body to write certain words. You stand aside and allow my intention to control your ego-body so that it sets the same machinery in motion to move *your* body to write them. So well do you put aside your own thought that though I write with your hand it is more or less in my writing. Also, neither you nor I can spell, which is a pity,' said Scott.

'And when I am working with Andrew he never allows me to make spelling errors,' I said. 'But do go on.'

'I doubt if I can make it any clearer. The process must be like this: My thought is transferred to your ego-being; modifications pass down by way of the controls of the motor-sensory nerves and so produces writing. I am thinking slowly in words and thinking them into written symbols in the usual way because I am imagining them actually written with my own hand. It's slow because it is a conditioning of my thought by your notions of time and by the necessity of feeling for words which are in your vocabulary.'

'I realise how tiresome this slowness must be but I do feel that when we need to be painstakingly accurate it is more sure than any other method.'

'I agree: hence my patience,' said Scott, at the same time giving me a comical picture of himself executing dervish-like somersaults in a perfect passion of *im*patience.

'It's all right now,' he said. 'I'm right side up again. I do agree that, apart from its slowness, writing is best when we need to argue out a subject and you must admit that I don't get nearly so impatient as I used to do.'

'But do be serious,' I said. 'It seems to me that mediumship is as yet in its infancy. As far as I can judge, seance room phenomena—materialisations, telekinesis, apports and so on—get one no farther. However these queer phenomena are produced they are only an appeal to love of the marvellous and they do not seem to lead to any serious investigation other than that into the honesty of the medium.'

'But you see, our theory of mediumship is not capable of proof until the constitution of the human body is better known and can be described more accurately,' said Scott.

There was a pause. I knew that Scott wanted to say something further because of the sense of urgency with which he nearly choked me but I seemed unable to catch on to his thought and my pen had to be pushed on reluctantly from word to word until the unaccustomed thought moved more freely into my understanding. With a great effort he got me started.

'To be convincing,' he wrote, 'the same information should be given at the same time to two or more mediums sitting together, but no two mediums seem able to make contact with the same person with any certainty. This is because differences in development, in astral make-up and in thought affinities are translated for us into actual differences in space. Thus, although two mediums may be at work in the same room on earth, they will have affinities with people miles apart in our space. Their contacts may even be with people in different planes. So that method of test is ruled out.'

'Oh,' I said, 'I am so glad you made me get that. I have often wondered why that particular test has not been tried and have puzzled painfully over the discrepancies when messages were received by two mediums working together. It shakes one's confidence badly when two quite honest people fail to confirm each other's communications and there is no way of deciding between them. But if the distance factor is decided by affinity they may both be right although they differ. I have always regarded the failure of this test as very damaging evidence against the genuineness of the whole business.'

'Then I'm glad I persevered,' said Scott. 'That painful doubt in your mind probably explains the reluctance you showed when I tried to introduce the subject. Remember, most of the people who are near to you on earth are really non-existent for me just because of this affinity factor. Their real presence in my world is elsewhere and I have no means of knowing just where. Superficial understanding of our conditions accounts for the whole difficulty. You were so afraid of bringing that doubt into the daylight that I could hardly force the words through at first. We must work for a clearer theory. There must be many genuine mediums at work and yet for one medium who is trying to understand the processes he uses there are many more who do not even scrutinise and assess their results. When mediumship becomes "respectable" there will be more chance of its practice going with scholarship and a trained mind. Then we may get some intelligent research into methods. Meanwhile, strict honesty and an open mind in the interpretation of the information we give you is the best for which we can hope.'

'Many people have psychic experiences and don't know what to make of them,' I said. 'They are puzzled and even ashamed of them because this materialistic age offers them only a pitying pathological explanation.'

'I know,' said Scott, 'and you make me very ashamed. I had certain queer experiences at times of great strain and was terrified because I took them for signs of impending madness. Also I had built up the kind of reputation which made me shy violently from anything "psychic" and so I missed the chance to reach reality by that path and had to wait until I got here. I have suffered for that avoidance.'

I waited for Scott's self-reproach to ebb. Then he went on:

'Thank you for being so patient and also for that thought. I *am* doing what I can in reparation for my fault. It is in no sense a punishment that is meted out to me, but the fact of not having developed certain powers that are needed here carries its own penalty. It is the doom of what one *is* and from that there is no escape.'

Chapter Six

Early in the history of my communications from E.K., we had discussed the problem of time. The measurement of time is for us tied to the movements of sun and earth, but there is a distinction between clock time and the concept of duration, which would seem to be an internal measurement, determined largely by the quality of consciousness. E.K. had always impressed on me the difference in the quality and meaning of time in his experience and he devised means of comparing our two ways of experiencing and recording time. We realised that the different quality of consciousness in his world must radically alter the conception of time especially as it was not regulated externally by the sun. E.K. also explained that whereas my sense of the present moment was of very short duration, his sense of 'now' covered more of both the past and the future and so gave to the passing of time an entirely new property.

I knew that his day was not marked off into hours of light and darkness by the turning of the earth and so was surprised when he made me understand that days were still used as units of time and that in their duration they coincided exactly with our periods of twenty-four hours. He had previously explained that our light had its effect on certain pressure readings in his plane and I now had to understand that the day of twenty-four hours was actually measured off by these readings. Starting therefore, from this agreement between our days E.K. suggested comparing the passing of time in shorter periods of hours and parts of hours, checking up with earth time by means of signals made to me.

First, I watched my earth clock and we checked off an hour of his time. Right away we found ourselves faced with a most unexpected result. The hours did not tally. We started off together but every time we repeated the experiment he signalled the ending of his hour about twelve minutes before mine had expired. Then we tried half-hours, only to find that they showed a greater contraction in proportion to their length. Thus, his half-hour finished in twenty-two minutes of my time. The quarter hour showed still more loss and ended for him when only ten minutes of my time had elapsed. We concluded that the proportion of loss increased steadily according to the shortness of the tested period. There was here what seemed like an insoluble contradiction. How could twenty-four hour periods agree in duration when the smaller periods of which they were composed showed this progressive contraction? We puzzled over these results and doubting our facts, tested them again and again but always to confirm them. All that could be done was to note the facts and leave it at that.

Attempts to compare distances had been equally baffling. Only one thing seemed clear; that space also suffered some kind of contraction. Any calculations of speed, involving both time and distance would of course be affected by the discrepant time factor but even so there was a definite contraction in space values. The whole thing was alarmingly difficult and made me long for the collaboration of a mathematician. But where find one who would credit my facts?

Scott commented:

'You have, of course, to take another dimension into account and it is probably the co-efficient of the new dimension which is upsetting your time comparisons. The fourth dimension, i.e. time, has been modified for us by a fifth dimension, that of degree of being. This last must vary as the measurement of frequency alters. It applies to organisms and is the scale by which their development is measured. Its sign is a differing quality of consciousness which runs up the scale from the lowest organism to man. In man each one of the degrees of being is represented because of his possession of all the grades of being from the etheric, which we agreed was the first remove from the physical, to the astral, up to the ego-being which is at present his highest element. But in man on earth, the consciousness that belongs by right to this highest degree cannot function fully because all the higher degrees have to be timed down to the physical and cannot free themselves to work independently until the physical body is shed. That accounts for the perplexing difference in your mode of consciousness and ours, and is one of the clues to this troublesome contradiction between your time and ours. So also with the comparison of space values; our different kind of consciousness makes our interpretation of phenomena different. The fact that our material world has an etheric foundation with a different range of frequencies from your physical world has something also to do with the differences.'

But E.K. had more to tell us:

'You must not stop short at comparisons for one plane or even for two,' he said. 'The facts to be considered are these: each plane shows this contraction effect for space-time values and it would seem that the sense of duration and extent fails to operate at all when the highest spheres are reached. Consciousness is such that *time and space*

94

become one and there is nothing that is not included in the eternal "Here", and "Now". We used to sing glibly something about "When time shall be no more" but we had mighty little idea of what we meant by those words. I begin to have an inkling of their meaning now and I take it that this kind of being is what is meant by "eternal life".

'I think there is no doubt that we all have the possibility of living in such a timeless present by virtue of the highest potentiality of our spirit. There are actually times, even in earth experience where a foretaste of this condition is known. Here, we frequently approach the experience and as we go on it will become still more natural to us.'

'You speak of the contraction of space and time,' said Scott, 'but don't you see that the statement is reversible? A contraction in space is only another way of saying that we can apprehend more of it at a time than you do and the same applies to time. So it amounts to a progressive enlargement of experience. Thus each plane should provide a vantage ground in regard to those below it. From the higher, one should be able to survey a larger area of time and space in the lower and if this is taken up to the highest, there must come a point in the series where the whole of earth experience in both time and space should be accessible from the one peak of being.

'Why, look,' said Scott, getting excited. 'It is like a cone divided into planes which contract as one goes up so that a larger plane beneath can be surveyed. Of course, height is merely symbolical; the contraction is an inverse way of showing the expansion of the area open to observation in the planes below. Do you follow? Also—and see how beautiful—from the higher places of the spirit observation of the whole of the lower ranges of being must become possible as time and space draw together into a vertex of

95

the absolute. Here we have an instantaneous survey of all time and space; the view-point of Omniscience.'

There was a pause after this outburst from Scott. Then E.K. went on.

'Wait,' he said. 'That is a wonderful conception but we have overlooked a vital factor in the situation. Each plane is separate as far as material phenomena go and the only activities which can be known beyond their own plane are those which share the frequencies of the planes beyond. These will be only the higher activities of emotion and mind so it is to be presumed that only such can be known by those on a higher plane. All that falls below their range of activities must be for them non-existent just as a great many of your activities are non-existent for us.'

'Yes: my symbol was too simple,' Scott said. 'Each plane must be able to know only its own kind of phenomena and experience is only transmissible above when it is sufficiently fine to reach the level of the higher plane activities. So to the Dweller at the Zenith only the highest in experience can be transmitted and the notion of the all-seeing nature of His knowledge needs to be qualified by the consideration of quality. What can go up is automatically selected by the possibility of its inclusion in the things that can be known on that particular plane.'

'That is rather a staggering notion,' I said. 'I am thinking of the human effort to reach up to God by prayer. If God must be thought of as what Scott calls "The Vertex of the Absolute" then your qualification of his idea—that only what is fit to reach so high can be known by Him—makes the success of prayer depend largely on spiritual development.'

'It means that to reach God is the final stage of an endeavour beyond the ordinary,' said Scott. 'It means also,

96

I suppose, that our prayers, such as they are, reach as high as they deserve to reach and no higher.'

'I fear so,' said E.K. 'But the potentiality to reach God is in every soul, remember. And why should one expect it to be so easy to reach God? On earth you have a fatal way of imagining that because a thing is desirable, it must be simple and easy. Yet it is only necessary to read the lives of the saints and mystics to know that a lifetime's discipline is necessary before one can find God. We neglect another important point here. The nature of God is love, and the simplest soul on earth may have enough love in themselves to reach up to the love of God.'

'What about inspiration in art, music and poetry?' I said.

'In these great adventures of the mind a man is developing and using the higher parts of his nature which thus enable him to make contact with higher spheres. These may be beyond him in time and space, but not in degree. If he can reach up and share in their experience he is able to bring it down and express it in terms of his earth life and so enrich the culture and tradition of his race. There is nothing like the joy of living at these high altitudes of the spirit and so the adventure is always, in itself worthwhile.

'The actual make-up of the artist or poet has to be capable of this advance development though,' said Scott. 'It may be rather an anticlimax but it means that even a poet's inspiration can be reckoned in terms of the finer frequencies of which his fourfold body is capable.'

Another communication illustrated the perplexing differences in our conceptions of distance and movement. E.K. said:

'I mentioned differences in our power of movement and

must try to explain. On earth, the movement of your body seldom keeps pace with your wish but here the hiatus between the will to move and the power to move is gradually closing up. The difference begins to be felt on the early plane where the lightness and resilience of the body make speedy movement a delight, but this is only a surface difference and directly I begin to try to convey the rest I am up against the dimensional problem in another form.

Velocity is a matter of distance and time. Now time has taken on a new disguise and is a stranger to you and so is the former. Even though I cannot prove my assertion, I will venture to say that there is a contraction in space. It has become elastic, compressible, variable. The will and desire operate far more in relation to its proportions. To say baldly that I can be wherever I desire is to give an over-simplified impression. Yet space has indeed become more relative to our consciousness of it. There is a kind of telescoping of near and far which answers roughly to that bald statement I made. The view I see when I am stationary is a plain data of so much space relative to me. I wish to be elsewhere and begin my movement in that direction. The scene dissolves and reassembles in other forms as I move and I am very speedily where I wish to be. I do not feel the rush through the air you are thinking of. My movement is in a space of my own which differs from that of the environment perhaps, because my position in that space of my own is largely a matter of my own will and desire.'

'Please stay a moment there,' I said. 'I want to realise the variation in two quantities we always think of as fixed —both time and space, which appear to have become variables. It is easy to say, but not to grasp. I suppose only experience of the difference would help.'

'I do not understand Relativity Theory,' said Scott, who

was sharing this discussion, 'but this might well be an illustration of it. "Different times in different cosmoses" Ouspensky quotes, and this is what seems to be experienced by us as though the powers of perception had caught up with the latest theories.

'It is probably more true to say that your theories on earth are catching up with our experience. I am tempted to think that some of these great scientists have been eavesdropping; they have caught impressions from us and with incredible labour have been able to express them mathematically. They fit earth-phenomena in right of its possession of the unsuspected dimensions which are proper to our planes.'

I had been pondering and felt that I had as yet a very poor notion as to the actual manner of the movement our friend had described. I asked him to enlarge on it. He replied:

'Even the actual experience is difficult to describe as a succession of events. Think of the overlapping of these larger areas of consciousness. This gives some of the future of one's movement to the present. It brings the future towards one as one goes to meet it. That is to do with the time factor. Now space, as I said, tells me clearly its extent in any direction but it also flows in towards me as I move, if you can accept this approximate description. This aspect of the scene dissolves as I go until the place I am seeking is reached. Do you remember thinking that one of the earlier dimensions might well be telescoped with others when a new one has to be added to experience? You thought of volume as being a compound notion and wondered whether it would be modified when it had to accommodate another dimension. It is tempting to wonder whether the case could be stated like that. Actually, it is quite bewildering at first, but the early plane gives one experience in a milder form so one gets used to it by degrees.'

'Is it as though the scene flashes past you like the illusion of a moving landscape from a train?' I asked.

'No, the experience is quite other. Directly I begin to note the wayside beauties or to direct my attention to what I meet I slow up to normal walking or even stop if the desire to go on flags. I should perhaps say that I find I have stopped. I must fix my will on the end of the journey if it is to be done in this extra-locomotive fashion. Now watch; from my hillside I look across the valley to a house on the other side, surrounded by trees. My immediate view shifts slightly, gets vague to me and goes through modifications by way of which it dissolves into this other. The distant house is now large and plain and I am standing at the door, having taken a dozen steps only. The dissolving of one view into another is not a sudden or startling experience. There is a sense of distance passing, a melting into one another of a panorama of aspects of the landscape but nothing suggestive of extreme speed. It is a very dreamlike experience, you think, and one would want to experiment with it a good deal before it felt safe? Scott realises that it has great fascination as a kind of inverse experience of speed. I am dissatisfied with this description but do not know how to better it.'

'If one were waiting for you at this other house you would not be seen to be coming, but would suddenly be there?' I asked.

'Yes, but remember that the people there would have premonition of my advance in the ordinary way, although they might not see me coming.'

'I want to know where your body is in the interim, when you are halfway, for instance.'

'It is *in* my body, in my personal space and quite safe.

It is where *I* am which is either at my own home or at this other. The space in between is not real space to me except when I am regarding it from one end. Then I know its measurable extent and could walk it in a set time.'

'Curiouser and curiouser. This is worse than fantasy; it is sheer miracle. What shall I do about it?'

'My child, you must cultivate a little faith, and if you can't do that, be content to wait and see for yourself. Meanwhile, Scott shall try for a theory, you shall try for faith and I will pray for patience, shall I?'

Chapter Seven

Andrew was less interested in the theory we were working at than in the actual structure and behaviour of human beings. His work, ever since he passed over in 1916 had been among those who needed help to adjust to their new life and for him the personality was of primary interest and importance. He was equally concerned for those who were his present companions and for those with whom I came in contact on earth and he was often able to help me to a better understanding of them. He explained that it was more difficult for him to diagnose the state of an astral body when it was masked by a physical form but he taught me carefully all that would be useful about the hidden processes at work in human relationships.

'It is easy for you on earth,' he said, 'to think of a man as being shut up within his skin and only able to influence others by speech or bodily action. But the hard outline suggested by the body is not typical for us; we see people as the centre of influences that ray out from them and affect all those within their range. In any case, the hard outline is misleading because in spite of it those same influences radiate from your bodies also and have their proper effects on those in the vicinity.

Think for a moment how these radiations are caused. Any change in the energy level of an activity causes it to throw off a wave of energy at that particular level. Physical atoms emit rays of their own frequencies; when etheric or astral substance fluctuates it also radiates waves of energy. The etheric substance of the body is especially concerned with life-processes and as it changes, corresponding influences are released. As you know, the etheric form is closely related to the physical and does not long survive it so it is difficult for us who have dispensed with it to study it properly. We have the third principle, the astral, as our outward form. During earth life this is only in process of development and is far less defined than the other two. It is the part of your organism concerned with emotions; it may be described as the total power to desire, and to feel emotions.

'If, during earth life, this part of the being has been directed mainly to physical desires and the satisfaction of material wants one is in bad case here where such satis- factions are out of reach. Now all these earthward-directed desires can become a torment and there can be no peace until they are re-directed towards more worthy ends. It is one of my tasks to help people over this difficult stage of longing for the unattainable pleasures of earth. It is only part of the harder task of making a complete adjustment to life as it must henceforth be lived.

'Whatever the state of the being at death, the giving out of some kind of emotion goes on continuously, since it is not possible to exist at all unless one has a "state of mind" and that really means a feeling-tone which streams out from the body in waves of varying quality. Fear, anger, longing, sorrow, disappointment, content, happiness, joy— one or more of these is constantly being felt and radiated out by every human being, alive or dead.

'("Alive" refers to us, of course,' said Andrew, 'and "Dead" to you).'

'How strange that is,' I said. 'But when you are talking to me I am aware of myself as being dull, heavy and somehow *dark*, which must be a reflection of your thought.'

'Don't be too depressed by the comparison,' said Andrew.

'We have all had to live in the darkness of earth conditions, and it is certain that you will all come sooner or later into our kind of light and life. You are not always so very dark, so be comforted.

'But let us come back to our subject. The astral body is visible to us in varying forms of light and these ray out from the body and surround it with its own peculiar atmosphere. The scope of these rays is limited to the immediate neighbourhood but within that range they may affect anyone whether the emotion is directed to them or not.'

'Then an emotion is really due to a fluctuation of the energy which makes up the astral substance and as its energy-level varies, waves of a similar nature are thrown off?' I asked.

'Yes,' said Andrew. 'The whole thing is a mechanical occurrence. It works by strict law for us all; but for you, the effects, both of transmitting or receiving such waves, quickly work down into the physical level and produce visible signs. You are frightened, shall we say. Your astral body retracts, changes colour and sends out a misty aura. Your etheric body registers these changes by giving you a pang of fear. (All bodily sensations are etheric in origin) Then your physical body receives the message and begins to react by altering blood-pressure and stimulating various glands. Your face goes pale and your breathing quickens So each part of the organism has made its characteristic response to the same stimulus.

'Meanwhile the ego-being is gaining control and deciding on a course of action. One can watch it gaining control even though it is itself invisible, by the gradual improvement in the pattern of the aura. Chaotic, swirling movement steadies down into a regular pattern. Suppose, now, that another comes along who has no cause for fear and

104

is anxious to help. His being is steady in its outgoing pattern and his light is strong and clear. Directly he reaches the first man his own light will flow in and begin to dissipate the foggy surround. The disordered swirl of emotions will gradually be re-ordered and composed. If the helper is strong enough (and that means loving enough) he will be able to impose his own harmonious rhythms and so completely calm the being of the other. Then you may see a lovely sight. All the energy which was locked up in the conflict of fear and anger is now set free and glows out into light and happiness directed towards his helper in love and gratitude.'

'I realise more now the direct impact of other peoples' emotions and what a real force they are,' I said. 'Even animals appear to be conscious of some human emotions, and fear and anger both seem to cause them excitement.'

'The higher animals have a well-defined astral body,' said Andrew, 'and so they are bound to absorb the astral rays you send out. They certainly respond to love and they have, for biological reasons, a strong reaction to the fear-anger group of emotions. Your fear aura will communicate fear to them and inevitably they will react with anger. Actually, the human reaction is just the same; fear excites anger, and anger, fear. The interchange of emotions is going on all the time in any human relationship and only your blindness to the astral rays you are giving off and receiving makes it possible for you to ignore the exchange.

'It is a lovely sight to watch the mingling of colour and light between two people whose relationship is a happy one. Where they are very close friends the two auras flow towards each other to create a common field of force thus heightening the individual power to feel the love and joy of both. Unpleasant emotions also spread around one and they tend to create a solitude which no one is anxious to invade. Anger, cruelty and malice inflict positive injury upon the bodies of those in the vicinity so if one is suffering from any of these nasty astral diseases one is left alone unless someone very devoted remains with one to try and effect a cure. It is no joke being a physician here but the fact that one has to experience in one's own body the illness from which one's patient is suffering, certainly makes for easier diagnosis!

'It is possible for you on earth to ignore the "state of your feelings" as being relatively unimportant. You think that only the state of your body really matters. But when the state of your feelings *is* the state of your body, and when, moreover, those feelings, being no longer dulled by the physical, are ten times more acute, it becomes a matter of the first importance that the state of your feelings should be healthy and happy. If you were suffering from an unsightly disease which made you objectionable to your friends and abhorrent to yourself you would take any possible means to cure it. That is literally the case with people who come here suffering from faults of disposition and temper, from fears and anxieties, from old angers and envies. For their own sakes, as well as for the sake of others they must be cured, or they cannot bear to live among us where their disease must be seen in ugly auras, harmful emanations or noxious odours. Besides, to see the full glory of a happy human being is to desire to possess it for oneself and in most of these unhappy cases cures are possible unless the astral body is hopelessly damaged by disease. Then the wretched being has to return to a lower plane where his unhappy body can be more easily endured. The lower astral plane where we all begin our experiences is the place for adjustment and cure. It is a kind of sorting house, a place of training and purgation to fit one for the more exacting conditions of the higher astral planes.'

'How do you set about the cure of people who are ill?'
I asked.

'First, one has to steel oneself to endure their atmosphere. To do this, one's own body must be in good order since it will have to absorb a certain amount of poison which will have to be neutralised. The curative agent is not a handy bottle of medicine: it is the healthy body of the doctor. I will try to tell you how I see it scientifically. All these radiations are the results of certain rhythmic activities. Where these are in conflict, as in the unhappy emotions, the rhythms given off are jangled and out of harmony. They therefore enter the body as painful shocks and dislocations of its own ordered rhythms. The healthy body has to absorb these disharmonies and to neutralise them. Now there is a scale of these rays and, as in physics, the finer and keener the rays the more they will be able to co-ordinate and control the faulty rhythms they encounter. They work in with the disorder and gradually smooth out its inequalities so that a new and better rhythm can be established. You will not be surprised that the finest, keenest ray of all is emitted when love is felt. This is the master-rhythm. It can sort out and re-harmonise every conflict in the astral body and it is our only means of cure. It may take many forms; sympathy, understanding and the will to help and heal. But these rays can only be given off by the healthy part of the astral body so while one's own nature retains dark conflicting emotions one is less effective as a healer.

'The emotion of love is not a special and separate thing; it is the *natural outflowing from a healthy astral body*. Nothing but love can be radiated from a body which is quite free from disease. The outflowing may take many bewilderingly beautiful forms, but only some form of love can be produced by the healthy soul. Don't imagine that any of us have as yet attained to that perfection. We know that it can be reached, we know of others who are nearer the goal than we are, but we know of none here who have reached it.'

'We have come to believe,' I said, 'that there are depths of emotion buried below the conscious level of experience and that it is difficult if not impossible to reach and influence them. Are you more able to see these hidden things and have they a visible form as well as the consciously felt emotions?'

'You are right in suspecting that there is much in the astral being that cannot be known consciously, but the underlying strata come gradually into consciousness here and it is the purging and healing of every level of the being which makes this process so long and difficult,' said Andrew. 'You will understand the full extent of the task when we talk about the many earth lives whose records are buried deep in the unconscious mind.'

'Apropos the painful effect of anger, envy and so on,' I said, 'I am beginning to be aware of their reality. It is quite disconcerting to have to feel the actual pain caused by such things when one would rather pretend that they are not real and only exist in the imagination. Obviously one cannot escape absorbing them into the body and, felt or not, they must injure the delicate substance of the astral being, I suppose?'

'Undoubtedly. The harm is the same even if it is not consciously felt. Moreover, the injury may work down by way of the etheric into the physical body and cause illness. Thus a child who is poisoned by dislike when it is craving for love is seldom physically healthy and, what is worse, it may develop serious astral diseases which will take life-times to cure. Many poor unfortunates who become criminals have been poisoned like this in youth.'

'Evidently it is time we stopped thinking that "feelings" don't matter and are only immaterial things,' I said. 'All this is very practical and helpful. Thank you, Andrew. You have given me personally much food for thought. How little one realises the harm that may be done by "venial" sins like impatience and ill humour. If we saw these things as ugly radiations and knew that they were actually hurting the bodies of others perhaps we should be more careful.'

Andrew added some further information about the emotions when later on we were discussing a particular case of some difficulty. He said:

'Wherever there is astral disease its primary cause is to be found in fear. Depths upon depths of it are constantly being revealed in the human soul. It causes a recoil into the self and the locking up of all helpful emotions in internal conflicts. A self-regarding attitude becomes habitual and one is tempted to condemn this as egotism. But if the fear beneath can be reached and relieved the whole system of recoil and self-imprisonment may be freed. Then there is an immediate transformation which can be made permanent by the reinforcement of confidence and courage. Never condemn selfishness or even malice as pure vice. They are the sign of a tormented and frightened soul which has recoiled upon itself and can only be helped by being set free from fear.

'I myself think that the discipline of earth is specially important for the following reasons: the actual emotional processes are masked by the physical and the strength of the sensations are dulled by it; hence, although fear of injury to the physical body is added to the dangers to be faced, yet the conditions do make it possible for each to fight his own fight while maintaining a bold face to the world. Here, no concealment is possible and the keenness of the emotions makes it a far more serious matter when anything is wrong with them.'

'I was thinking,' I said, 'that all the good institutions and influences on earth aim at softening and ennobling the feelings. Aristotle's definition of tragedy is that which purges the emotions, for instance. Then the appeal of religion is to right feeling as well as to right belief, and music has its direct effect on the emotions, as art has also by other methods. All these must contribute to releasing and conditioning emotions in the right way.'

'Yes,' said Andrew. 'I think that the task of building a happy and healthy emotional body is peculiarly the job of one's earth experience. I am glad that the emotions are beginning to be more studied. You have the teaching in the Gospels, as in all inspired religions, "Love is the fulfilling of the law". I want to write for you a detailed analysis of the processes of the astral body as we know them here, but we must make that a separate piece of work.'

Scott had followed all this with interest and here he brought us back to the field theory of matter which we had previously discussed.

'I should like Andrew's opinion on this: density in a universal field of electro-magnetic energy gives us physical matter; density in yet another universal field, that of etheric energy should give us the etheric forms of plants, animals and humans, and so also density in a universal medium of astral energy should give the astral forms of animals and men. The ego-being is invisible to us and harder to understand, but it is probably the most powerful of all the fields of force represented in the human make-up. Can the field theory justly be extended to cover these finer kinds of matter?'

To which Andrew replied:

'We think it probable that the universe is built up on this graded scale. The earth itself is certainly interpenetrated by an etheric field and this again is shot through with astral substance. The ego-principle eludes our observation but it is probably related to a universal sphere which is our medium for contact with all degrees of spiritual beings. I think you can take it that the field theory is as true for the higher kinds of substance as for earth matter.'

'Then we have two aspects of truth to connect,' I said. 'First, there are the four interpenetrating substances in a man's body all geared in together to work as a harmonious whole. Secondly, each of these substances is related to and continuous with its own special universal field of force. Man would appear to be a complex area of density in four fields of force at once and this region of complex activity is his body, physical and spiritual. One must no longer think of him as a being separate from his world, an independent organism clear of control or influence and nicely segregated in a body. He is a kind of tangle, or knot in a continuous pattern woven in fourfold fashion throughout the universe and is thus in contact with all its fourfold activity. If this could be realised and acted upon, it looks as though man might learn to wield extraordinary powers as yet undreamed of.'

'That will serve us for a summary,' said Andrew. 'Do you remember that we were speaking of a field of astral force created between two people when there is intense emotional activity? It is quite plain to see that a sudden heightening of the power to feel means an increased vibration in the astral substance. The change of rhythm causes the outflowing of a wave of emotive power which has the effect of heightening the vibrations of the astral body that receives it. Even in an earth body you feel the faint indications of this glowing into keener life. That is why emotion is desired. It increases the feeling of being alive. It is literally "fullness of life". That is why people run after any kind of sensation or excitement. Social intercourse is a constant give and take of this living influence. If the weaving patterns of astral light were visible to you it would not be difficult to picture men as concentrated patches of denser astral substance in a world of astral light. That is the way it actually looks to us.'

'I wonder how one relates this to modern psychology,' I said. 'This postulates a reservoir of emotional power which it calls the libido. This branches out into the primal instincts of self-preservation, sex, and power. It is only fair to say that the psychologists are not agreed as to their order of importance but the interesting thing to me is that there is never any attempt to locate this emotional centre in any part of the body.'

'That omission shows a sound instinct for the truth,' said Andrew. 'The libido is just another name for the astral body so there is no need to quarrel as to the precedence of the types of emotion when one realises that it is the feeling-aspect of all the activities possible to a body and mind. Feelings are simply agitations set up in the astral substance. Agitate atoms and they emit rays with an intensity related to their own frequency. So with the waves set going when an emotional disturbance sweeps across the organism. *These waves are free to travel in their own kind of space,* that is, in what we were calling the astral field. They are free to enter and influence any organism with an astral form. After all, you admit that light rays are absorbed by the skin; you go further and realise that X-rays penetrate the body. Now you must add that astral rays spread through the astral body and are absorbed by it.'

'But how is one to find evidence of these processes?' I asked. 'Not many people actually feel these exchanges and lacking experience there seems no way of proving their existence.'

'Perhaps not,' said Andrew. 'But you see, this kind of knowledge is in the air. And that careless phrase is truer than I realised because it is literally in the universal ego-field and pressing hard for an entrance into human thought. Modern writers are urging their readers to experiment in psychic development and more and more people must be proving to themselves that there are states of heightened consciousness which it is within their power to feel. Such people should begin to experience in themselves the reality of emotional exchanges since these will be reflected in actual symptoms which they will not be able to ignore. You remember how painful some of your earlier experiences were and how you suffer even now when hostile emotion is directed towards you. I think that an account of these effects might be useful to others who are undergoing similar development,'* Andrew concluded.

In obedience to Andrew's suggestion, I set down here some account of experiences which must be familiar to many mediums and sensitives.

In the course of my work I found that the interchange of thought with my friends is always accompanied by its appropriate feeling-tone. This serves as comment and illumination to the exchange of thought. These emotional discharges are received as distinct sensations of a pleasurable or disagreeable kind. They enter the body as keenly-felt vibrations thrilling through its substance. Some ex-

* Cf., De Chardin's concept of the Noosphere.

perience is necessary, however, before one can realise their full meaning. The pleasurable feelings such as excitement, joy or love thrill through the body as waves of beautiful sensation and their progress through the being is clearly felt. The important thing to note is that they are received as physical sensations and not emotional ones, and that their meaning in terms of emotion has deliberately to be attached until experience enables one to interpret them. Thus, one may receive a flow of joy or a stab of anger and in neither case may one be aware of the source or cause unless meaning reaches the thought at the same time. This is proof to me that emotion, unless it is winged with meaning tends to work back on to a physical basis.

However that may be, the pleasurable emotions have a good effect and produce ease and health of mind and body. They must, I think, feed the astral body and keep it content and happy. They are felt as an easing of physical pain and as a benediction to the whole organism. Where one receives them consciously they are so invigorating that it is easy to understand their efficacy in faith healing practice. It is increasingly plain to me that in a real sense we feed upon this healthful exchange and are poor and starved without it.

The opposing group of emotions, impatience, fear, grief and anger are painful and disagreeable to a degree. One begins to dread and avoid them whenever possible. Anger burns like a physical flame, fear is a choking fog in the throat or a cold dis-ease of the whole body and grief is a keen hurt, aching and intolerable. The mixed nature of sorrow is plainly felt as a blend of love and grief probably because it has generally an element of self-pity which is confused with love for what has been lost. All of this group are felt in the nature of the gesture that would accompany them. Anger is a thrust, impatience a fever, fear a creeping paralysis and admixtures of any of these produce a painful agitation of the whole being.

Yet these emotions from other people are received, not *as* emotions, but as sensations. Thus to receive a pang of anger does not in the least arouse anger in return. The anger simply hurts the astral body which apparently reflects its injury down through the etheric and physical. It seems clear that the harm inflicted is due to inharmonious vibrations which have a jarring effect on the body, upsetting its normal rhythms and so causing real suffering. Just as the receipt of good emotions acts as a tonic, so bad ones cause injury.

Antidotes to evil emotions come to be known and used as experience increases. Love will smooth out any vicious vibration, speedily over-ruling it and tranquillising the body again. I have sometimes been in pain because I have picked up a dose of anger, when someone has directed love towards me and the ease-giving vibration has quickly neutralised the pain. Quite by accident, I discovered what a marvellous curative agent we have in laughter. I had been badly burnt as a result of meeting bitter anger and Scott made one of his irresistible jokes. Perforce I laughed and my pain went as if by magic. The mere feeling of amusement brings relief at once and this gives an indication of the true nature of humour with its necessary ingredient of love. I have been studying these emotional exchanges over a period of years and I am sure that to know them physically is to gain a valuable insight into their real nature as actual agents for good or evil in human affairs.

As to origin, all emotions are felt more keenly when they originate with those on higher planes. We, who are still in physical bodies can neither transmit them so strongly, nor get their full effect in receipt. But quite perceptible sensations come to be felt when the emotions originate with people on earth, and quite a lot of inconvenience can be caused by the physical symptoms arising from anger, fear, envy or impatience. I am convinced by my own experience that there is this real interchange of near-physical reactions between us at all times whether these are expressed in acts or words or are only felt in the mind. Even the emotions buried in the unconscious may have their due effect. To feel these things physically is to add to both the pleasures and the pains of living, but the experience is worth while because of the added understanding it gives of the real nature of one's fellows.

Andrew commented thus:

'But you can only experience in muted form what is a poignant interplay of feeling for us. Remember, your emotional has become our physical and it is bare to the extreme sensations of joy and sorrow. Your emotional exchanges are dulled by interaction with your material body which tones down everything for you. But since we experience keenly and nakedly with our astral selves naturally we transmit feeling to you in a more powerful form than anything you are used to. Your way of experiencing these sensations stresses the dual nature of the exchange. In the outgoing process an emotion originates in a rise in the level of being, literally a lift into a higher velocity. If the emotion is an undesirable one it is transition into a chaotic mode, due to the conflicting rhythms of two opposed emotions which as your body receives them will spread disharmony throughout its substance. The transmitter of the emotion translates his feeling in terms of meaning as you do. Thus we say "I am happy" or, "I am angry" or, "I am sorrowful". These changes in rhythm are transmitted, not as meaning but as vibrations which travel a restricted distance at a definite rate. Any organism, human or animal may receive the wave of astral energy and consciously or unconsciously will make its appropriate response. There is a response to each emotion as purely automatic as the response to physical stimuli; only by exercising ego-control can this reaction be avoided. You are never immune from influences from your fellows. Even though you are insensitive to them your astral body has to absorb them.

'Every man, then, must carry about with him all the time his own emotional atmosphere. He is a powerful centre of influences which stream off from him and affect all within his orbit. There goes a red thrust of anger, there a pure beam of love, there a sparkling ray of fun, and each must be absorbed by the astral bodies of those he meets. You are blind to these exchanges, but there is no way of hiding our feelings here. They are all proclaimed by the visible colours and patterns of the aura. It is a pity that your real emotions are so easily hidden on earth since you can deceive yourselves that they have no effect unless they are outwardly expressed. But you must reckon with this: in the actual raying out of your own harmful or helpful emotions they are bound to have tangible effects on others and when you cannot understand their behaviour, it may well be a deeply instinctive response to your real but hidden attitude to them. Their unconscious mind may realise and act upon its knowledge although they never become aware of the real reason of their attitude to you.'

With this warning Andrew ceased, promising that at some future time he would help me to work out a fuller description of the psychic aspect of emotional disturbances. 'It is a subject of which I have made a special study,' he said. 'I want to examine your psychological doctrines in the light of our knowledge, but that will be a full-sized job and rather outside our present aim.'

Later on, Scott and I had an interesting conversation on

the subject of the transmission of thought. The typical ego-activity referred to as 'thought' must not be confused with intellectual processes of calculation and reasoning. It is an intuitive activity concerned with the world of meaning. It deals with 'forms' in the platonic sense. He said:

'I was interested in Andrew's explanation of the travel of emotion which differs from the travel of thought. This is a far more rapid process suggesting that it moves through a swifter medium. If emotional waves are released by the astral body then thought waves must originate from a finer source of energy—the invisible ego-being itself, which must be able to transmit rays which travel at enormous velocity and which appear to have no limitation of range. We were told that the speed of thought was instantaneity as though it had eluded the space-time system altogether. This links up with the time-space speculations when, if you remember, we saw that the vision of the Highest must be of the whole of time and space in "here and now". If that is too difficult, never mind.

'There, in the thought projections of the human ego-being we have something which links us to the activities of all the mighty beings of the higher planes of existence. Who shall say how much of the pure thought of the seeker after truth, be he saint, seer or scientist, originates in these higher spheres and is picked up and interpreted in human terms by men on earth? I think this may be why a new idea sometimes seems to spring to life in the minds of men in different places at the same time. I think it probable that thought is not a strictly individual activity at all but that each of us takes from a vast common stock, a freely flowing ocean of thought waves. We simply select the thoughts for which our times are ripe, and which suit our individual attitude to life and the stage of development reached by our civilisation. The range of thought waves appears to have no limit, which is another way of saying that they escape our notions of space and travel in zero time. After all, the highest earth-speed, that of lightwaves in a vacuum is a purely arbitrary limit else why should just that particular number of miles per second be a limiting velocity? That it is so for the physical world is certain but the fact leaves a query in the mind like a piece of music which does not finish on the dominant. This can't be the end of the matter, one feels and I think that the final degree of being which we call the ego-principle must have standards which cannot be expressed in human terms—that of the speed of thought, or instantaneity. Notice that if things began to happen at this rate, the ordinary method of thinking of one thing after another, which constitutes time, would be quite useless to us any more. We should have to be able to think of everything at the same instant of time and where would time be then? You think I am teasing you and so I am in part. But these sort of conjectures interest me greatly since I understand better now the possibilities of altering the aperture of consciousness and increasing the experience that can be taken in at any one time. Our increase in scope is really due to the shedding of two mediums which dragged down our speed and kept the aperture of consciousness small. Having attained greater speed I see the possibilities of continuous development along the same lines. Too difficult for you? Let us stop, then.'*

* Received in 1944. Note the anticipation of De Chardin's.

Chapter Eight

'Putting together the evidence we have accumulated so far,' said E.K., 'we conclude that in the course of ages matter acquired the power under certain circumstances to add to its modes of activity. It began with a purely physical mode like that of a mineral substance. Then the plant developed the life-mode and so has an etheric form interpenetrating the physical. Animal organisms added the astral mode to the other two and in man a fourth mode emerges, that of the ego-being. Each of these emerging modes of being has its own special functions. The physical produces chemical reactions; the etheric is responsible for growth, sensation and reproduction; the astral is the medium of desires and emotions and the special province of the ego-being is thought and meaning.

'These modes are related to certain planes of being but in your spatial reference they all operate in the universal space which is all you recognise. Actually, space is *not* one; it is a complex of many kinds of space each with its own typical frequencies and each of these modes of being has reality in a space of its own. This differs in dimensional values from all others and, for its proper denizens, remains a separate world. Thus there are planes of being based on etheric activity where the etheric mode prevails. The planes we inhabit now are known as the astral planes. Beyond them are others but not in any different space, but with their warp interpenetrating that of all the others. Thus all being is one and yet it is distinguished by its possession of all, or less than all, of these modes of being. This is, of course the real significance of the planes of which you hear so much. Now perhaps it would be helpful to put this in tabular form.'

Modes of Being	Degrees of Being	Typical Activities	Typical Beings	Planes
Physical	1st Degree	Chemical & Physical Reactions	Minerals	Earth
Etheric	2nd Degree	Growth, Sensation, Reproduction	Plants & Unicellular animals	Etheric & Transition Planes
Astral	3rd Degree	Desires & Emotions	Animals & Men	Astral Planes
Ego	4th Degree,	Thought & Meaning	Men	Higher Planes

'These modes of being pass insensibly into each other,' E.K. went on, 'and are linked by intermediate stages. Man, as the highest organism has the four interpenetrating modes while on earth. In the transition stage he has three, having shed the physical. He then leaves the etheric behind and in the astral planes he has only the two modes, and as he progresses he is finally left with only the highest mode, that of the ego-being itself. This is his ultimate simplification.'

Andrew added the following comments:

'Just one warning. Neither of these four modes is independent of the others. All of them develop in graded fashion. There is not one simple astral body, for instance, but a series of forms in that kind corresponding to the several astral planes we inhabit as we become fit for them. May I add a word about each of these modes of being?

'The etheric is very near to the physical body. It is the

"life" form which alone gives sensation and power of growth and reproduction to what otherwise would be only an aggregate of mineral substances. Actually, in the course of growth, we have the queer phenomenon of the etheric body anticipating the physical as though it set the pattern by which the body was to grow. In man, the etheric is very fully developed and very deeply sunk into the physical so that it has very little power of separate action. Where an individual is found with an etheric body less sunk into the physical there is more tendency to be aware of the life of etheric and astral planes. There are cases where it is shaken loose by shock or overstrain. Then queer states of consciousness are apt to be experienced—hallucinations and visions which may be reflections of events in other planes, chance glimpses that cannot be related to earth experience and are therefore regarded as pathological symptoms. But normally the etheric is so closely knit to the physical that it never works loose even in sleep. It takes the final shock of death to part the two.'

'There is a thing in ordinary experience which may be of the same nature as the visions you mentioned,' I said. 'I mean those queer visions one gets when on the very edge of sleep and which last just long enough to be grasped and remembered.'

'Yes,' said Andrew, 'that is interesting because it probably shows the drawing apart of your modes of consciousness as the sleep state is established. These glimpses of strange things may be due to the separation of the astral-ego beings from the other two principles. It is as though their withdrawal exposes the edge of the astral consciousness with its reflections of other states of being.'

'They are not dreams,' I explained, 'and yet they have no connection with waking thought. It is as though one slipped into a kind of middle gear from which one can either come back to full consciousness or drop into sleep. Bringing back these half-way impressions one is somehow aware that they are part of a continuous experience and that they would make sense if one could only get hold of the context. Ordinarily, we do not pay any attention to them, regarding them merely as precursors of dreams, but when one attends to them they make an absorbing study. At the cost of a little effort I think nearly everyone can observe these visions and the experience is very pleasurable. I recommend it to anyone suffering from insomnia; one looks forward to the process of falling asleep and is sorry when oblivion cannot be held off any longer.'*

'Let us try to understand what happens, then,' said Andrew. 'As the sleep state is approached, the astral and ego bodies detach themselves from the physical-etheric which remain inert upon the bed in their usual close relationship. Now your edge-of-consciousness impressions are probably a selection from astral experiences, traces of which may be apparent to the astral being as it detaches from the body. You say these visions give pleasure and that means a necessary connection with the astral body which is always involved in any emotional experience. I think, too, that it is a sign of emotional well-being if these halfway states are happy. In cases of astral disease or ill-health they might be expected to be painful or frightening.

'Although this experience must be affected by etheric influence since there is an incomplete separation of the modes, it does give you some idea of the kind of consciousness which is born in one after the transition period here is over. At first, you see, it is a very incomplete, twilight awareness and one has to get accustomed to using it before it rises out of the dreamlike phase. Then it is a

* A full study of 'hypnagogic hallucinations' is given in my *Fourfold Vision*.

123

totally different type of consciousness from yours. You think that because I appear to speak to you in words such as you yourself use, I therefore think and speak as you do. This is a false impression. My normal mode of consciousness is different; my normal mode of expression is different too. When we talk, I have to slow up my usual process, push an idea towards you as it were, and grope about in your mind for words with which to clothe it. You often take in and act upon ideas I send to you without being at all conscious of their origin; I often accept ideas that come from *your* mind, or perhaps I should say, via your mind for no one knows where ideas really originate. The world of thought is free and we pick up from it what suits our train of thought. We select from a world of thought which is common to us all, either on earth or here with us.'

'Then you would say that your world and ours are closely connected in the thought mode of activity, less closely in the feeling mode and hardly at all in the life mode. The physical, of course is quite cut off.'

'Yes,' said Andrew. 'Thought is a universal mode, feeling is restricted in range and the other two forms of activity are still more confined to their own spheres. But think for a moment of the influences, good and bad, that man attracts to himself out of our spheres of being, simply because of what he is in his astral and ego being. He cannot avoid these influences reaching him; they are bound to obey the law of affinity. So a man bent on evil is continually assailed by evil thought, an "earthy" man may be influenced by elemental beings of earth, air and water who are attracted to him because of his enthralment to earth, while a man of higher spiritual development can share beauty and holiness with the highest beings of all.'

'Does this mean that good and evil can be thought of as entities apart from good and evil men? If they can affect

124

us without the agency of any personal beings it looks as though we must do so.'

'Evil thought operates freely, as I have said, and there is this excuse for projecting it into imaginary forms, such as devils and wicked angels. But don't forget that evil has a *limited source in evil minds*, whereas good is the universal foundation of all being. So the sum of evil is always limited whereas the sum of good is infinite and it is always pouring into creation to absorb and neutralise the evil.'

'Then there must be a varying amount of evil mixed with the good influences in the thought world?' I asked. 'I am thinking of times when war is widespread and all forms of wickedness seem to flourish.'

'But since evil is a negative, conflicting form of activity it is bound to be overruled and reharmonised by good,' said Andrew.

'How does it originate, if the foundation of things is a principle of love and harmony?' I asked.

'That is a deep question. I shall only say now, that in order to become manifest, being must have two aspects, a positive and negative in opposition. We speak of matter as activity, but no activity could be apparent to the senses, either yours or ours, unless it acted in a medium which provided it with opposition. It has to have a background of inertia, if you prefer to think of it like that, or no one could possibly be aware of it. It would spend itself effortlessly in a void and there could be no such thing as matter. So all substance, all separate being, depends on the interaction of these two principles working in an accurate balance of power. Where this balance is upset and the negative gets the upper hand we have the beginning of evil, since unbalanced opposition breeds anger even in the rock which will respond to a blow with a spark. As soon as the organism is in question, all the gamut of emotions based on fear and anger come into play and as they invade the world of consciousness they acquire an independent existence in evil thought. We shall have to understand this more fully later on but I wanted to give you some notion of the way in which what we call evil may originate from purely natural causes.'

The writing ceased and although I waited for some time, Andrew had evidently no intention of developing his interesting suggestion as to the origin of evil. I found myself recalling his words in the details of everyday life, as I battled with a blustering head wind, perhaps, or struggled to move heavy and awkward objects. I realised for myself that when one is met by this impersonal negation of purpose, anger and impatience are generated. Even if they are controlled for the moment, it is likely that they will find vent perhaps as hasty and unkind words to another, which in their turn will produce an angry reaction. So in practice I began to check up on this process and to realise how much evil we may all set afloat in the world of thought even in the course of our peaceful daily routine.

Chapter Nine

Once one accepts the fact that life is indestructible and that we as living souls are embarked upon a process which has no end, death and birth, usually regarded as opposites become simply two aspects of the same event. One goes through a door; that is, one dies to the life on this side and is born into that on the other side.

'This business of going through doors, of dying and being born again on the other side is a necessary condition of our continuous life and has to be repeated again and again,' said E.K. 'One goes through the door of death; a physical body is left behind and all the rest of the being goes through. One has then a short interval in a kind of anteroom and here another body, the etheric, is left behind. This is the second death. Then yet another door opens which lets us through into this glorious world of the astral planes where a long period is usually passed without further change.

'But the purifying and developing of the new body into which one has now been born eventually alters its texture and in course of time it prepares for another change. This time "death" is less a matter of throwing off a useless husk than of gradual change into a new form and a gradual transition into the realities of another plane. And so it goes on, death and birth becoming more like each other each time until in the end they become literally the same thing.'

'That first transition interests me,' I said. 'Will you tell me in more detail what happens then?'

'The etheric is too close to the earth rhythms and would

prevent us leaving the earth plane or putting away earth ways of living if it was retained,' said E.K. 'It has to be shed before we can enter the astral planes. While it is loosening, it fills the mind with a rapid survey of all that has happened during a lifetime. The etheric is a necessary vehicle for the clear-cut, detailed earth-memory and as the real being draws away from it, the record of that memory is exposed. This is a strange interlude, as others have told you, but it closes in a deep sleep during which the etheric body is finally shed. With it one loses the detailed memories of events that are passed, although their traces in the emotional body remain and can be recovered. But this is a very different kind of memory from the accurate mechanical one due to the interplay between all four modes of consciousness during earth life. So do not wonder at our difficulty in producing the sort of evidence of identity which seems so important to mediums.

'In the case of a man who has died normally—after an illness or in old age—after the passing of the etheric body he wakes up conscious of his surroundings in the astral world. His degree of consciousness will depend on the condition of his astral body. It may be a very new born, helpless body at first. This precious, delicate thing with its fluid, flamelike texture, has been the robe with which the physical has been clothed during all the soiling activities of earth. All the hopes and fears, joys and sorrows, angers and miseries of a lifetime have left their mark on its sensitive substance, making or marring its form for use in this, its proper world.'

Here Andrew joined us and took up the theme:

'What I want to emphasise is that in the undeveloped soul the astral body is inclined to be formless with un-developed organs of sight and hearing and may be quite incapable of living on our planes. Such people are born here in utter helplessness and a long time must elapse before they are strong enough to live normally among us.'

'What can the ordinary man do to help himself to avoid this trouble?' I asked.

'Any amount, if he knows how,' said Andrew. 'Even without special knowledge he can be well prepared for the change if he leads a decent life, is morally sound and not too selfish. He may still have a period of helplessness to go through and he will regret his ignorance for many reasons. You are thinking that one should be able to give definite instructions to aid development but I am doubtful about this because they could so easily be misused.'

'Mustn't one risk that in such an important matter?' I asked.

'I am not sure,' said Andrew. 'The methods of occulism —thought control and the disciplines of prayer and meditation are good, of course, but the trouble is that I am an extrovert and I distrust the introspection which is bound to go with conscious development.'

'Certain people will always be introverts, and if their activities were directed they might be useful instead of harmful,' I said.

'Yes, that may be true and as we can't all be happy extroverts it may be well to suggest ways of developing along sound lines. But what is that thought? No, I saw you hide it so you may as well come clean.'

'Well, if you must have it, I agree that extroverts are usually happy people but I do think they are liable to be shallow.'

'That is the wrong word, I fancy,' said Andrew. 'The quality of which you are thinking is really a good one. These are probably younger souls who have had less of the painful experiences of earth to shadow their outlook on life. You see, personally I like these younger, less sophisticated souls just because they are simpler and easier to help, but there I am giving way to prejudice and ignoring the finer qualities which age and repeated earth experiences can give to the soul. We must talk about younger and older souls another time because you don't fully understand what is implied by those terms. You and I are bound to differ on this point because we represent different types.'

'But we are wandering from our subject which was the possibility of development during earth life. The astral body is helped into growth by such things as meditation and controlled thought and these will give it the rudiments of astral sight and hearing. But it is more important to consider the *quality* of the astral substance you are seeking to develop. Any bad emotional habits, such as tendencies to anger, greed, selfishness or cruelty are signs of disease in this substance. While there is a diseased condition present in your astral body it is highly dangerous to attempt development since it will accentuate astral illness and may lead to madness and death. In any attempt to develop the astral being, emotional soundness must come first. You would not attempt to train as an athlete while you were suffering from intermittent fever. You would first cure the fever, then wait for the body to recover strength before subjecting it to the strain of strict training. So with the astral body. It too must be in a state of health before it can go on safely to further development.

'Christ followed this course with his disciples. That little band of close followers had to be developed up to their full capacity, but if you read the Sermon on the Mount you will see that the first emphasis was on their moral training and that it was designed to purge them of fear, hatred and anger and to clear their souls of disease by the practice of love.

'You remember the awful storms of emotion by which you were shaken in the early days—the welling up of unbearable sorrow and hopeless anger at the injustice and cruelty of life?'

'Yes, only too well,' I replied.

'They were due to premature development. You had repressed certain emotions for so long that you had seriously injured your astral body and the penalty when the damage made itself felt was shocking.'

'But now the storm is over I don't grudge the suffering it cost since it brought us together again and made it possible for you to find and help me.'

'I know that you have never grudged the suffering, dear, but I want you to realise the risk for others. Emphasise always that the preparatory stages of initiation must be thorough or catastrophe may follow.'

'The fear of those days—not so much the fear of the experiences in themselves but fear of an uncomprehending world, took a long time to die. It has only been vanquished as I learnt to understand my own experiences and to master their lessons. It is this knowledge that I want for others.'

'It may be wrong of me to hesitate,' said Andrew, 'but you see that anyone who enters deliberately on a course of development must reckon with the release of repressed emotion and probably with the emergence of what is locked up in his unconscious conflicts. It is impossible for him to know beforehand of what nature these may be. If he is aware of the appalling strength of these forces he may be better able to bear their release with fortitude and to control the existing situation.

'But even granted the knowledge of one's own emotional problems, there are other dangers as you know, though in your more prosaic moods you are apt to scoff at these as fantastic. I wish so much that I could make you see that there is not a word in the accounts of Christ's life and teaching that is without significance. When he talks about men being possessed by evil spirits he means precisely that and nothing else, and when we water down his meaning by pretending that he is simply using the customary notions of his age and that they can therefore be interpreted in modern terms, we are discounting a real danger.

'There *are* weak, malicious spirits here, who have never got beyond an elementary development and who are only capable of mischievous activities. Normally they cannot reach the consciousness of men but when emotional disturbances accompany development they are attracted and will attach themselves so as to influence the person in wrong ways and to accentuate the suffering of both mind and body. Now to know this may be dreadful and it may alienate the prosaic and scientific mind but I am afraid that does not alter facts. *Now* do you still think we are justified in laying people open to such experiences?'

My answer was yes, and for two reasons that seemed to me to have weight.

'All experience is good, and none should be refused out of fear. Then, from a less selfish standpoint, if one knows the conditions and is warned of the danger, is it not possible that such weak and vicious spirits may be helped?'

Andrew agreed, although I could feel that the conclusion still troubled him.

'Certainly the great thing is to face the risk with open eyes. As you must admit, one may lay oneself open to fierce temptations and it will be necessary to resist thoughts, feelings and images of an undesirable nature. If I could have made you understand my warnings in time, much of what you suffered from such causes could have been avoided.

'As to helping these poor souls, it can only be done in the way you know. When their influence is felt, one must not shudder away in fear but accept their presence and try to understand them, since they too were once human. If they can be induced to feel any good emotion so that the body they have almost destroyed can begin to function again they may be able at last to take that so-long-impossible step upwards and be saved.'

'I am trying to relate this to the structure of their bodies,' I said. 'I suppose they still have an astral and ego-body?'

'The astral has gone into reverse, as it were,' said Andrew. 'All its reactions are negative and hostile. The substance of their bodies is wholly of the lower astral kind and it may be badly injured and diseased as well. The ego is there but it has become an instrument of antagonism to life. Such beings have lost the power of constructive living and care only to spoil and destroy. This lamentable state is never the result of one poor life experience but of many, all on the downgrade. Can you see how almost impossible it is to arrest this downward tendency?'

'I get an awful picture there, whether from your mind or from elsewhere,' I said. 'I see that once that negative attitude is taken it will automatically make one an enemy of society and will bring down upon one penalties which can only embitter the soul and drive it still further downward to its doom of ultimate stultification. Then, driven out of our world in a violent or cruel way one will come into your world seething with the sense of one's wrongs and mad with hatred of one's kind. Is there *any* hope for such a one?'

'Steady, dear. Go back to what I was trying to explain.

The astral has two principles, positive and negative. These poor things of whom we are speaking have lost the positive and are only capable of the negative emotions. These are the shadow side of light, the negation of all love and virtue. While this state remains one is only capable of a twilight existence on the lower astral plane and this is not a happy place. One cannot leave this plane until the balance is altered and positive emotions can be felt. I would not dare to say that any creature in this God-founded world is hopeless, but to reach and help these poor things is for us an almost impossible job.'

'How awful—how inflexible the moral law is when at last it has to be seen in physical terms,' I said.

'Yes. It is no longer any use to fall back on vague generalities. A man stands or falls by what he is and he can only exist in the plane for which he has fitted himself. There is simply no escape from what one *is*. It has to be seen and known of all.'

'Then I say that this is a terrible world and that we are like blind and foolish children playing with forces we don't understand and subject to dangers—appalling dangers, we are not capable of seeing. Why are we not taught and warned?'

'Steady, dear, steady. We *are* both taught and warned but like children we disregard the warnings and refuse to be taught. Take every opportunity of giving the warnings for if you neglect any you will not be free from responsibility.'

Here Andrew ceased, probably driven away by my unfortunate spurt of anger against an order of things neither simple nor pretty to contemplate. I was left confronting a law of necessity against which I saw that it would be childish to rebel. Yet I did rebel against it and could only tolerate the thought of it when I reflected that this could not be the last word and that in the infinite love of God, some saving love must reach even into these depths of despair.

There was more to be said about the purgation process and E.K. took up the account.

'Soon after shedding the etheric body and waking fully on the astral plane,' he said, 'one's thoughts begin to be much concerned with the life of earth which has been left behind. The clear-cut memory has been lost with the etheric body, and yet, as one begins to use the astral body and it grows in strength, the scenes and events of the past life begin to come vividly back in terms of their *feeling* content and in a manner never experienced before. In the course of one's life on earth, experiences are reflected in consciousness and one never doubts that one has realised the whole of them. But the impressions of people, events and acts which now come crowding back are far more real and comprehensive than when they were actually experienced. The difference in this presentment of the past is that included in it now is the reaction of other people. I find this difficult to explain. Everything that happens to you affects others as well as yourself and every event has therefore as many aspects in *reality* as there are consciousnesses affected by it. Each of these others concerned in these events had their emotional life altered thereby even though you were quite unconscious of what was being brought about by your agency. Now, in this process of recollection, as an incident comes back to one's mind it brings with it the actual feelings, not of oneself alone but of the others who were affected by the event. All their feelings have now to be experienced in oneself as though they were one's own. This means that the effects of deeds on the lives of others must be experienced as intimately as though to do and to suffer the deed were one. Where sorrow and wrong have been inflicted, sorrow and wrong must be *felt*, not merely known to exist.

'Most of our deeds on earth are performed in ignorance of their real bearing on the lives of others. There may be an uneasy sense that others are involved in suffering because of us but we often choose to ignore this. We have understood a situation with our mere intellect and have kept back sympathy which is the beginning of knowing in oneself what this suffering is. So often we have remained in ignorance of the real events we have set going in the lives of others and these things are now gradually revealed to us as a part of our *own* experience. Where sorrow and wrong have been inflicted, as I said, they must be felt. We have to face the reliving of our whole earth experience in this way.'

'That is retribution of such a deadly justice that it makes earthly justice look like mercy,' I said.

'Not only is it justice,' said E.K., 'but it is redemptive suffering. It breaks up once and for all the hard core of selfishness and cruelty which earth life often forms and which would make a man unchanged in this respect an immense misery to himself and his world. It is a purely natural process, set going by the astral body itself which thus works to rid itself of impurity and disease. All these things which it has to re-live have been real events in the astral world and so are a part of the unconscious experience of the astral self. As this is our actual, visible body now, and its reactions are no longer veiled by the physical, we have to know them intimately and the moral law is set for us now in physical terms.

'Now the detailed memory is lost, as you know, but this does not prevent me having a fuller knowledge of the real significance of all I did on earth. As I re-live it, I find it to be at once better, and worse than I knew. I saw it before "As through a glass, darkly, but now face to face". I am only in the middle of this retrospect myself and have some way to go before all my earth experiences have been seen and known fully in the light of reality. I judge that by this process one is gradually emancipated from earth and, having repented and accepted the truth about oneself one is free to continue in other spheres the proper development of the being.

'You must realise that all this recollection does not take place in a void; it is the subjective side of life and the ordinary objective living goes on with it side by side. Of that exterior side we have spoken before. It is a full and happy one unless the retrospective process is too fraught with suffering.'

'Andrew, I suppose, has finished with this retrospective stage,' I said. 'He was only twenty-five when he died and that was a long while ago. I expect I was catching his thought there for here is his writing.'

'Yes, it is I,' said Andrew. 'I have been waiting to claim your attention but I would not interrupt that very good explanation. The retrospective process is certainly the dickens for us all and I imagine it is the fact behind the Roman Catholic idea of purgatory. There is no doubt that it does purge the evil of earth life which has to be faced in its full reality, accepted and then left behind. It is true also, that where the life has been definitely evil the process is longer and more awful. There is remorse, and plenty of it, even for a man who led a short and fairly blameless life. It is not often possible to make amends here when one finds out how one has injured others; the opportunity has gone. Most earth connections have to be loosed or dropped at least for the time being. So there is the beastly thing one has done and it must be known now for what it truly was without any of the eyewash which one used to use so liberally to cover one's uneasiness. Anger against oneself is useless and shame and guilt come to be known as false attitudes due to pride. There is nothing for it but to accept the thing and recognise one's full responsibility. Sorrow must be curbed for the sake of others around who would have to share it, so all one can do is to be humble about it. In effect one says: "Yes, I did that. I am *like that,* more's the pity. I am not the fine fellow I thought myself, but now I will eradicate that fault, strengthen that weakness, clear out that anger." It becomes a process of stripping off all the pretensions with which one deceived oneself and others and of facing at last the real man. Very small beer he is too, when one actually comes face to face with him.

'When this purgation is fully accomplished earth life and one's responsibility for all one set loose in that current of cause and effect can be laid aside. More difficult matters begin now to claim one's attention. We work here with an ego-centred consciousness and an astral body which means that emotions are our physical manifestation and intuition is our mode of consciousness. The retrospective process purges the astral which is now our physical body, clears it of conflicting emotions and makes it a worthy vehicle for the transformed and developing ego. The last stages of retrospect fittingly close in the innocence of childhood and one thinks that at last there can be peace and a sense of all scores settled.

'But it is rather like coming to the end of a long tunnel and suddenly finding an extensive view opening out ahead. For now, beyond birth the great perspective of past lives begins to open up. They are distant and they have not to be lived out in detail as one's latest life has been but

138

they begin to come clearly into consciousness for acceptance by the ego and for inclusion in the sum total of
experiences which have built up the personality.

'Now I should like to tell you about this past but I
think your instinct to wait for such knowledge is a sound
one, and so I refrain. For myself, there is no harm in
saying this much. You have not come into my life until
this last incarnation but you will do so again, and that
suffices me.'

Here we passed for a time into talk of a personal nature.
Our separation and all the suffering it had involved for
both of us had come into focus now; we had accepted
it and could lay it aside. As Andrew said:

'There is no sorrow in this now because I can see more
of the past into which the whole experience fits and more of
the future which will complete it for us. I trust the God
we both know to bring this relationship of ours to its
perfecting in some as yet unforeseen way.'

There was one statement Andrew had made which I
thought called for explanation. He had said that earth
connections had often to be dropped. This had disturbed me
and now, at my request, he went on to make the matter
clear.

'This business of finding people has never been fully
understood between us. People become widely scattered
as they find their true affinities here. I can't always find
M— now because she is content to stay in the early stages
partly because she feels at home there for the time being,
and partly because she is waiting for F—. I can find her
thought; yes, in much the same way as I find yours, and we
often talk together. As to others who are here and to whom
you would like to speak, that is sometimes more diffi-

cult since I have no means of contacting their thought. You must remember that distance depends for us on affinity, so it is difficult to get in touch with those with whom one has no earth connection. When you are with their friends and I happen to be present in thought, I can sometimes get a direct lead to them. Of course, an intentional message could be given. You must remember that we are separated into planes of being and unless we happen to be close to one another here the only way of finding a person is by tracking his thought. This can only be done if one knows what lines to try. Urgent thought of the one you want often attracts his attention, and then contact can be made, but if one does not know the person it is difficult to send out the right thought or to recognise a response if one gets it.

'You see, our lives are not devoted to guide activities as they would need to be if you were destined to that work. We think it is *not* your work and I know that in this you agree. Our interest is in the more general psychic truths and while we discuss these we attract the kind of thought which is also concerned with them. Quite often useful help reaches us from unknown sources, as you know; all thought is one and like attracts like.'

'Yes, the sudden appearance of a different handwriting on my page is always an adventure and often the unexpected contribution is a crucial one. But I am still a little vague about the possibilities of communication. Am I to understand that it may be difficult to keep in touch even with one's nearest and dearest if they are not at the same stage of development as oneself?'

'Affinity and equal development constitute nearness for us and their opposites mean that we are parted by actual spatial distance. For instance, you and I may have to wait a time before we can be literally together on the same plane unless you achieve a good development on earth and so catch up. We shall be closer than we are now, of course, but it will depend entirely on you whether we find ourselves on the same plane. But get a sense of time, not in proportion to your short earth spell but in our sense; then you will realise that we shall have long ages of time together before we have to return to earth. We must take a long view of all human relationships. Wherever the course of life brings one into intimate contact with another it is probably one's destiny to renew that relationship at some future stage. You and I have much to do together. Our lives have barely begun to touch as yet and our association may take many forms in the future.

'While we are on this question of differing stages of development it is well to remind ourselves that "the last shall be first, and the first, last". What we often take for difference in worth is nearly always a difference in age, and in actual fact, the less developed may well have the higher potentiality for growth. But it will end in the same way for us all, sooner or later, and I see the meaning of the process as none other than the perfecting of the whole race. Eventually we shall all arrive at our goal as the pure, equal and joyful children of God.'

Chapter Ten

'Andrew has given us a useful account of the astral body
which is his special study,' said E.K. 'Let us go on now and
try to understand the work of the ego in connection with
it. As he has said, the ego is invisible to us and although
that may be an accident of the vision possible to our plane
I think that as yet it is a very formless principle. For even
the astral body is largely unformed during earth life. It is
clear that the ego has a larger scope and almost unknown
and undeveloped powers but even its present activities
are remarkable enough. It has the strange power of standing
off from the other bodies and of regarding their doings
objectively. Thus we say "I feel happy" separating the "I"
from the feeling of happiness. That is the ego looking at
the astral almost as though it belonged to someone else.
Then we say (or *you* do) "I feel tired" and that is the ego
considering and judging the sensations of the etheric level
of consciousness.

'In spite of this tendency to stand away from them, the
ego also identifies itself with the other bodies in order to
claim for the whole man his separatedness from the environment and it is remarkable that neither the astral nor
etheric beings can perform this act of separation for themselves. They exist, and they live a life of feeling and sensation, but they cannot divide the self from the not-self.
Animals, whose highest principle is the astral body, share
with men the life of the etheric—the sensation life, and
the life of emotion by right of their possession of an astral
body, but experience for them is an undivided whole. They

are part of their environment without a break. To an animal feeding in a field, the wet grass, the motion of his tongue, the taste of the food and his movements in search of more grass are all one experience centred in himself. He is not in the field, but the field is in him. It is from this undifferentiated mode of experiencing that the ego divides us. We know ourselves as entities separated from our environment and can even get outside our own sensations and regard our own thoughts as objects of knowledge. It is hard to estimate the effect this power has on our capacity to live fully. It gives a keen edge of joy and fear to all our sensations as well as lengthening our awareness in the forms of anticipation and recollection. At the same time it gives us a unique mastery over our environment because it is no longer a vague part of ourselves but something exterior which can be overcome and used.

'The ego principle also acts as a co-ordinating principle. Each of the other forms of body has its own type of consciousness. There is the blind body-consciousness of the etheric, and the pleasure-pain, desire-purpose consciousness of the astral but it is the ego which gathers up all these partial consciousnesses and achieves their concentration upon the focus of attention—that little, lit patch of experience which is the conscious mind regarding the present moment.

'The ego has achieved this clear focus of attention but this is only a beginning. The area of the patch thus lighted up varies from man to man and for us the loss of the cramping physical and etheric forms results in an increase in the area of consciousness. Our present awareness takes in more of both past and future. I think the ego principle is only just dawning in man and that as it takes fuller possession of him it will extend his power of knowing by gradually conquering more of time and space and bringing it into the present light of actuality. Ego activity has affinity with high spheres of being and it has an invisible and universal character which transcends the little barriers of the self which, nevertheless, owes to it all its illumination.

'This, man's most spiritual principle, directs its activity in two directions: it works inward to spiritualise the lower bodies and outwards to find contact with its own proper world, the world of meaning and reality from which it is largely cut off by its segregation in the flesh. Its inward work begins with the astral, or emotional body which has to be educated, controlled and formed in healthy and beautiful ways. Next it should gain control of the etheric and so be in command of all bodily functions. When this stage is reached there will be no more disease or illness since the body will be fully controlled by the mind. It is likely that when this state is attained it becomes possible to exercise a beneficent influence over the bodies of others. But very few men have ever reached this stage. Most are still at the beginning of the endeavour to bring the emotional body under control.

'The other work of the ego-principle is to infuse the whole of experience with the special value we call *meaning*. Thus, purpose grows definite only because emotions have meaning. This work of the ego upon the astral being is the beginning of the shaping of the astral substance into its proper form, and it is this work, well or ill done, which makes or mars the soul for its after-death existence. It is only too obvious that the ego has just begun on this task since so often the emotions have the first and last word in every decision and all the ego does is to mask their control with rationalisations. But the process is well begun in us all although we shall need many more lifetimes to perfect the work.

'The ego also has to use the etheric activity. Without

144

its agency the etheric brain could only reflect its record of changes in the chemical substances of the brain, to which the astral consciousness would give merely a confused set of "feeling" reactions. No clear thought or perception could emerge unless the ego was present to translate all this into terms of meaning. One sees a tree, shall we say; that is, the physical reactions caused by certain vibrations in the etheric brain which are picked up by the astral in terms of pleasure-pain, but the meaning of the thing called a tree has to be supplied by the ego-principle. It alone can relate the reactions of the other bodies to the world of meaning, which is, in effect, the only real world. Apart from these connections with reality made for us by the ego all perceptions would be seen to be the illusions that they really are. A misty unreality would pervade the whole world of perception and feeling.

'In themselves, the processes of reasoning would go on in the etheric brain like reactions in a computer but they would be devoid of meaning and as automatic as a piece of machinery. Memory, too, without the intervention of the ego activity would operate in a purely mechanical way. It would be able to reproduce an experience with its associated feeling tone (astral record) but it simply would not mean anything at all. The ego alone deals with the world of meaning and although it can and sometimes does give wrong meanings to events, it at least deals with sense data in a meaningful way.

'Notice that in trying to recall a memory, the ego initiates the process. First comes a vague "meaning" impression and this serves to re-activate the vibrations which the original experience set going in the etheric and astral substance. These vibrations, once established remain active in the brain as long as it exists but they cannot again become part of conscious experience unless they are found and lighted up by the ego, and re-translated into meaningful experience. In "trying to remember" the ego beam has sometimes to search for quite a while before it finds and illumines the appropriate vibrations. How do we know when memory has brought back what we are looking for? The answer is that the ego has ways of knowing which are not revealed to the conscious mind. It knows the answer all the time, but cannot transfer it to consciousness until the old vibrations are found. Consciousness is always dependent upon the concerted action of all four modes of being; it cannot function for any one of them in separation from the rest.

'I can tell you nothing about the substance of the ego-body. It is seen to alter the patterning of the astral, but, as I have said, in itself it is invisible. The spiritual world to which it truly belongs is an invisible world, unless, as I suspect, it may take a form of light which we shall be able to see when we have reached its own purity of substance. It is the only world where the imperishable essence of all things abides. All visible bodies change and are superseded, because they are only the temporary creations of the world of meaning and so must be outgrown and put aside. But the wind of meaning blows through them all the time, altering and patterning them, so that, even though they themselves are illusion, they serve to carry for us the values of this higher world.

'I am often brought to a condition of worship by the wonder of the progress by which man obtains entry into this world of reality and when I get glimpses of this eternal life which has thus become a possibility for us all I realise that the suffering which seems an essential part of our training and preparation for it is a very small price to pay.'

'You are meaning that "eternal life" is not a matter of duration in time, but of the quality of being?' I asked.

'It means both,' said E.K. 'One is dependent on the other. When the higher powers of the being are fully developed and the lower conditioned and purified, this kind of intense living becomes possible. It means too, that if one can attain to this degree of development one will have become capable of living for a time in the lovely realms of light where every form of body will have been finally discarded and one will live in the effortless joy of the spirit. To attain this eternal life means among other things the possibility of spending a much longer period here before the descent to earth must be made again.

'Meaning is grasped by the use of a power which is peculiar to the ego; it is what you mean when you speak of intuition. By this I do not mean a mere guess at some rather fantastic aspect of probability but a most essential part of the mental make-up of every sane person. We should cease to be men without it and we should become less even than some animals who already show signs of dawning intuitive powers. This capacity varies from man to man since it is a rapidly developing power, but it should be an almost piercing awareness of the *meaning* of things. Its exercise brings great satisfaction and joy as though the use of this almost godlike power carried with it a higher zest and exhilaration than can be known by the use of any other human faculty. Poets and artists and all creative geniuses share this peculiar joy and it compensates them for all the suffering that a high degree of ego-development often involves. It is only possible to work creatively when one has an intense apprehension of meaning, because it is the effort to translate meaning into tangible form which constitutes creation. In my terms, this means that the ego-vision is so intense that it works down

147

into the emotions and produces a passionate love and desire to bring to birth in actual form something of the vision known intuitively by the spirit.

'Intuition is at work all the time, even in everyday life since a just appreciation of meaning must come before any invention is made or can be used. We should be unable to understand any of the physical facts of life without it. It enters largely into all our relations with our fellows in business, work and play. In the moral, aesthetic and ethical values which we, as men are able to appreciate, we see the work of the ego-consciousness. Where it is poorly developed the man approaches again to the animal level of purely astral activity, and for him the loveliness of nature or of moral grandeur or ethical worth cannot as yet exist.

'When consciousness operates on this level of being, the level of reality, it is almost set free from the bounds of the personal life and loosed into the freedom of a universal mode in which self-consciousness is temporarily laid aside. It has to come back into its segregated life as the scope of being contracts again, but during these excursions into the universal realm the ego experiences the peculiar joy of release. The golden bird, cooped in the cage of its own individuality, shut off by the barriers of personality from its home in the open skies, spreads its wings freely in the pure air of its own heaven and for a while flies out into the unconfined world of beauty, truth and goodness. The pull back into the body is strong, however, and not to be resisted while one is on earth. Yet the higher the body one inhabits the easier it is to remain free of it. As body after body is shed and at last the ego alone remains as the sole bearer of life, it will no longer have to bear the pain of separatedness from the universal life and joy which is its birthright. It will be free at last to remain in the realm of eternal life.'

148

Chapter Eleven

E.K. was waiting with impatience to carry on the theory of the fourfold nature of reality to its connection with rebirth. Now the way seemed clear.

'I am satisfied,' he said, 'that the process of development and growth apparent in all organic matter makes rebirth logically necessary. Any process has to be thought of as a never-ending sequence of causes turned effects and of effects becoming causes, as we said before. You may think of any such natural process petering out on earth but that is because you see only what goes on in your own sphere. The energy you lose track of is to be found here again in a different form. Nothing escapes from the total world of experience; that world must contain what it held in the beginning of time and will hold forever more. The only difference is the manifestation of that energy either on our planes or on yours, and its continual evolution into new forms carrying more of the meaning of the Creator.

'I begin to see that the purpose of God is the creation of meaning and that every creature has its own unique contribution to make to this. The vast manifold of the universe whirls and vibrates in a bewildering variety of forms only to this end and we ourselves are involved in a series of recurring lives by means of which we shall perfect the unique personality-meaning which is to be our special contribution to the whole.

'There is struggle in the process. Without the complexity produced by conflicting forces I doubt if there could be activity at all; no matter, no form, no separate beings. In fact the universe would revert to the formless and in-create; the world without form and void.

'But let us examine events as they affect a human being. We shed our physical body when we leave earth; we shed the etheric body when we enter the astral plane; we shed the astral body in its early form when we ascend to the higher astral plane; and finally, the astral body itself must be laid aside when the ego, sole surviving principle of the being goes on to live in its own sphere. And what then?

'Two possibilities present themselves. The first is that this ego-being when clear of all its other forms may be sufficiently of the nature of God to be absorbed into the universal life of reality. Or, secondly, if the ego is not perfect enough for this it must reach a stage in its ascent of the planes which will mark the limit of its powers to ascend. Then the highest it can reach at the limit of its powers will decide its fate. Beyond this it will not be able to go; its course in this cycle of existence will be finished.

'Now if the first possibility, that of absorption into the very substance of God were to be likely it means that at the crisis of my fate I shall find in myself the power to know God. Moreover, I shall have to be completely clear of all entanglements with earth, to have settled all scores with my fellows, to be utterly clean from guilt and pure and perfect in my inmost spiritual being, since this is the only part of me which will be left. It is only necessary to en-visage such a state of affairs to realise how far one is from its attainment. In fact, I doubt whether we know how near we still are to the beginning of our course and how many ages it will take to clear and spiritualise every principle of our being so that at last it is fit to be set free from earth. You see, this purifying process must be ex-tended to what your psychologists call the unconscious mind and down to its most dark and dismal depths before the man can be really clear. The conscious mind is nothing. Behind it are the records of many past lives and their tangled consequences have to be brought into order and harmony before the inner man is purified. Even for the best of us I see this consummation as aeons away in time, so for ordinary folk like you and me the possibility is so remote that we need not consider it.

'Now for the second supposition, that I may exhaust my potentialities and so can go no higher. This means that I shall have thrown off every conceivable sheathe and shall be reduced to a single, simple substance and mode of being. I shall have arrived at the ultimate simplification. My body will be of the nature of the ego itself, pure spirit, unsupported by any material form, even the most ethereal. I shall have become nothing but essential meaning, an enduring pattern in rhythmic vibration perhaps, but no longer a visible being in any sphere. My body, if one can still speak of it as such, will have become just the residual *idea* of the characteristic behaviour which expressed my personality. It will have no further power to progress because the inward self has now become the outer man. Varying lengths of time will be needed so to strip the being that it is reduced to its simplest and highest terms but eventually each of us must reach that stage.'

'Why, having reached what would appear to be a purified, effortless simplification of being, should one ever seek to return,' I asked. 'Why come back to the flesh with all its struggles and complications and have to begin the process all over again?'

'I do not suppose that question can be fully answered by anyone who has not reached that crisis of his fate,' said E.K. 'I certainly am a long way from it and so cannot speak with any authority. It is possible that at this time the vision of the whole journey of life is complete and that the soul, looking before and after and summing up its tale of good and evil, realises that no further progress is possible without another descent into the flesh. I know also that there are many spiritual agencies at work to influence the spirit to do the will of the Creator and so it may be that the decision is not left to the man. He is still imperfect, even if he is purified of fault; that is, he has not yet achieved his full meaning. It is possible that he may go back of his own will, but there is probably much guidance given to the descending soul by great spiritual beings who know how to lead the returning ego back to its fated place in the scheme of things.

'Many affinities will draw him to his rightful place on earth; many obligations unfulfilled, many attractions not yet fully explored. The pull of sympathies, of place, of race will decide his parentage and place of birth. This belongs to a study of the whole theory of rebirth, to fate, or karma, which is nothing mysterious but simply the working out of the purpose and meaning of the whole series of lives he has led or has still to live. It is this total meaning which controls all experience and so karma is only a way of expressing the purpose of God for any particular soul, and the permanent allegiance of that soul to the purpose of God which it is his business to work out through each succeeding incarnation. For one life-cycle is only an episode in a whole; the same meaning runs through it all, informing and influencing each lifetime. What looks like blind fate is nothing of the kind when it is seen in relation to the whole. It has its real meaning as part of the whole and serves the purpose of the whole. In fact, there is nothing in any life that can justly be called fortuitous.'

'You actually mean that all the things that seem like

blind fate, all the stupid, accidental things that hinder and hurt are not just the work of exterior cause and effect but are really obeying some kind of mysterious inner necessity?'

'Yes, I do mean that. There is no such thing as exterior fate. Every apparent accident is an essential part of the pattern you have been weaving in life after life and though some events may seem to break in and disorder what looks like the settled order of a life, that very disorder and the consequent re-setting of the pattern are justly related to the larger design which includes the tale of *all* your lives. Every incident in life has its true significance only in relation to the series as a whole.'

'Then some day I shall understand all the crass and stupid things that have broken in and spoilt my life, as I now feel. I shall realise why I have made stupid mistakes and had to pay so dearly for them and better still, I shall understand and appreciate more all the good things that appear to have come to me by pure chance.'

'Yes, there has never been such a thing in your life, or in any life as pure chance. Life is far too impregnated with meaning for that to be possible.'

'What about freewill,' I asked. 'Is that also an illusion?'

'No,' said Scott, suddenly taking a hand in the discussion and startling me by the impetuosity of his dash at my pencil. 'I think that the weight of precedent exerted by the course of events in a past life does have its bearing upon the present life and that the happenings of the past do tend to repeat themselves in slightly different ways under the new conditions of the present. But freewill means that one either does or does not break away from the compulsion. Freedom, which is a different thing, consists in the power to carry out the unconscious aim of the being without undue interference from the environment, but

153

this unconscious aim is really the result of all one's past lives in their influence upon the unconscious mind. This does not mean that one is obliged to follow the same pattern of behaviour in each incarnation. It only means that, given similar circumstances, one is *likely* to do so.

'Where the pattern has been a poor one, the recurring of an old and familiar situation may become an important crisis of fate which will decide more than seems involved in the simple decision one makes. Suppose, for instance, that in a previous life I have gone mad with anger and killed a man. In my present life I am suddenly confronted with a similar situation. There will be a strong tendency for me to repeat the pattern as before. If I succeed in avoiding this repetition either because of better training in this incarnation or because I have really progressed in my own development, I shall have overcome my fate and shall avert the ensuing pattern of disaster which has previously spoilt each of my lives. I shall have altered perhaps permanently what may have been a recurring design in many of my past lives. My will, you see, will have acted freely to contradict the pattern of the past and to set me free from it for good. In my view there is always a choice between possibilities, only this choice is biased by a very strong pull from the past. I think there is no question that the patterns do tend to recur and that the problems set in one lifetime which prove impossible of solution then, may be solved more easily in the different setting of the ensuing life.'

'Yes,' said E.K., 'I agree in the main with that. We shall understand this more clearly when we can recall the full story of our previous lives. Then the continuous meaning and purpose will dawn clearly upon us. Scott is probably right. He begins to appreciate the intensely meaningful quality of earth life where even the most trivial incident has its place in the weaving of an age-old design.'

Here Scott again took control; the writing squared off and was more deeply scored on the page. He said:
'I want to work out the physical side of this "return" theory. I take it that when one's bolt is shot there is very little left but a formless idea of a man, a kind of essence distilled from one's whole series of lives. Now there seems a break here in the *necessity* of the process which I don't like. Up to this stage each change has been the result of a self-determined event. It has been due to the operation of law and has not depended upon a man's arbitrary desire or choice. It has pleased me, just because one step has led of necessity to the next in as cool and reasoned a way as in a laboratory experiment. Now, suddenly, we are left with no sanction for the next step. *Why* return?'
'I will tell you how I see it then,' said E.K. 'Remember that both you and I must have travelled that way back to earth not once but many times before and therefore that record of the return must be graven into our spirit. As we have been saying, these recurring situations must exert a big pull and tend to repeat themselves.
'Then also, that pattern we call personality is precious and for every individual, unique. Now when one reaches this last stage is there a danger of the loss of this individualised meaning—that it tends to thin out and disperse into the universal life? Bound up with its being now must be the knowledge that the process is unfinished. God is not satisfied. Life is being defrauded; the end is not yet. Here then, is the spirit at the confines of being, judged by itself and judging itself. It has reached the promised day of judgement and until fulfilment is reached, the verdict must be, "Return, ye children of men". It is a fearful

and critical hour in the spirit's history. We do not often speak in religious terms, since they take too easy a path to a conclusion. But I want to confirm the Christian teaching at this point. The Christ Spirit is evermore concerned for the fate of mankind. He has, by His own life on earth, identified himself with that fate. His influence is strongly felt on each plane although His spirit has affinity with spheres of being so far beyond the human that it would have lacked the power to mingle with our life and to redeem it but for the connection made by His incarnation. He is "God with us" all through this ascent of the planes and it is to Him that the spirit in its last crisis must turn for help.'

Andrew interposed to say: 'I endorse all that and am glad that you can accept it.'

'So at least the spirit in its extremity is taken and led back to earth. Don't mistake me there, Scott. It would of its own will take the plunge back into matter when the critical moment arrived. But in resigning oneself into the hands of Christ there is a sense of security which the spirit in itself has lost and so the sleep of birth overtakes the ego and it is guided back. The man, as a thought of God, re-enters matter. He abandons all. Even his sense of identity is gone and nothing remains but the formless ego with its inherent power to refashion its bodies in conformity with the essential meaning it has brought back. Now, etheric, astral and physical bodies all have to be born again and the moulding agent is the ego.'

'Still not quite satisfied,' said Scott. 'Your assertion that the Christ Spirit is responsible for the return seems to me arbitrary. One has to take it on faith alone and although I admit the necessity of faith I think that it is a pity to invoke it at the end of a logical sequence of arguments.'

Scott's dissatisfaction evidently influenced E.K., because

the communication stopped there and Andrew had apparently deserted us as suddenly as he had come.

Later in the same day I was returning from a walk when my steps were hastened and I was propelled to my writing table with the indecent speed which usually meant that Scott had something urgent to say. It was not Scott, however. My pen began making great curves forming by degrees a mounting spiral. At the final, smallest curve I had the queer illusion that the whole corkscrew was collapsing, flattening out. The mounting spiral was a familiar symbol for the ascent of the planes and I supposed that the last curve represented the reduction of the being to ego-simplicity, but why the collapse?

I sat and stared at the paper and as I waited, I sent an urgent thought summons to E.K. Presently he was with me. He was on to the meaning immediately.

'The end is automatically the beginning,' he said. 'There it is then. At the beginning of each cycle the Meaning of God enters matter; at the end of each cycle it is again reduced to the simplicity of its beginning and is ready to combine with the physical embryo. It is only when it is thus reduced to this state of pure spirit that the embryo can combine with it. Utter simplicity enters utter innocence. "I am Alpha and Omega, the Beginning and the End." That is strictly true then, necessarily true, and a profound fact in the story of our cyclic development.'

Here for some time we stopped. There was much to ponder in the truth conveyed by the symbol. It was the keystone of the arch we had been building and I know that we all rejoiced when it fell so miraculously into place. Later on, E.K. commented:

'I am still resting happily on that conclusion. The beginning and end of man are nearest to God in terms of pure meaning. Alpha and Omega. Isn't it wonderful how aptly these drawings are given when we, with our silly reasoning, can get no further. I can see now what fogged us: the notion of height. We kept on thinking about reaching the highest point of development and of the *descent* to earth as though it was literally a long way between the two. We have been warned so often to ignore this height dimension. I could laugh when I think of the diagram collapsing so as to teach us in a way we could not mistake. There *is* no separation in space, of course. It is merely a separation in degree and where the degree becomes the same, as in the reduction to ego-simplicity one is back on the same plane. So when the ego becomes pure spirit, this brings one back into the scope of the newly created embryo and makes incarnation possible, and indeed, inevitable. Now I hope Scott will be satisfied.'

'Yes,' said Scott, 'I'll pass that. I caught your excitement and came. This is grand. It links up at last. Reduction to simplicity is essential since the degree of being thus reached is the only one that can possibly recombine with the physical. It has a necessity now that I couldn't feel before. Of course there is a good deal of mystery still left. I think there must be on the part of the embryo a corresponding attraction for the returning spirit as though it had need of this principle and so was ready to absorb it. I am really delighted with this. We have now the outline of a natural and inevitable process and this, I feel, was demanded to complete the theory.'

This piece of work gave us all the utmost satisfaction. The swift and urgent meaning conveyed by means of a drawing had been used as a method before when the topic under discussion had defeated our combined efforts. The delicate drawing reproduced here was one such. It came while we were thinking of E.K.'s quotation: 'And sayest, return, thou children of men.' It has for me a very moving

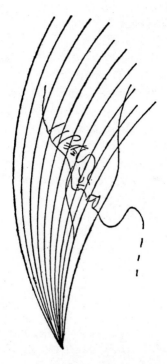

'And sayest, Return, ye children of men.'

quality. But now we were all impressed by the simplicity
and effectiveness of this latest symbol. It was evidence to us
of a mind with which we were sometimes able to make
contact; a mind which worked swiftly and surely among
realities but which no longer cared to express its meanings
in the clumsy medium of words.

Scott took an early opportunity to go back to the subject.

'I want to hear, E.K.,' he said, 'how you think the ego
works to reshape its vehicle. It has entered a bodily form
but not one of its own providing, since in itself it is the

result of a long physical process of heredity. The ego has become an unconscious spiritual principle and yet it carries long associations with a personal past, with a corresponding tendency to repeat the patterns of its earlier lives, as we have said. The interaction of the two, ego and physical form, each with a different heritage from the past looks like a very complicated business to me.'

'There is no doubt about that,' E.K. answered. 'I think it certain that the embryo cannot develop without the presence of the ego. The ego is probably responsible for building up the etheric form out of the general etheric substance. On this model, as Andrew has said, the resulting physical body will be formed. The matter out of which the physical form has to be shaped has potentialities due to heredity and only within the limits set by it can the ego influence the making of the body it has to inhabit. To be as accurate as I can, the interaction between the etheric, built up by the ego and the physical, modified by heredity, will give the resulting earth-body. It is a vitally important matter, since this form will endure for much longer than an earth lifetime; it will last for the whole of that cycle and its make-up will thus influence the being for perhaps hundreds of years.

'The etheric body seems to anticipate the growth of the physical child all along and to be only partially sunk in the body up to the time of maturity. Then the physical catches up and finally absorbs the etheric form which from that time is lost in the physical—completely interwoven into the same living structure.'

'I think it is possible that the ego has the last word in this body building process,' said Scott. 'If the physical follows the indications of form set by the etheric then the ego must be striving all through the time of growth to reproduce something like its old form in a past life. This throws a singular light on some of the problems of heredity. A purely physical theory of mathematical re-shuffling of genes in the chromosomes is not adequate to account for the spiritual side of our human heritage, although it may go far to explain the physical aspect of the child. In other words, although the ego-personality has to submit to the strict limitations set by the hereditary physical body-pattern, it will strive to modify this throughout the period of growth.

'The etheric spreads out and around the child's body and is a more fluid medium for the influence of the ego to work upon. The physical body follows the more developed etheric and one can imagine the fine balance thus established between the physical pull of heredity and the ego tendency to repeat its own peculiar personality pattern. The looseness of the etheric body in childhood gives the child a power which it will lose as the etheric sinks more deeply into the physical. Have you ever noticed the eyes of a child and how much more they understand of the immaterial world than is given to an adult? The child is continually catching deep meaning from its involuntary contact with the etheric world about it. Its faith in fairies, gods and miracles comes from this contact and will be lost as the etheric sinks deeper into the flesh. I think that a certain looseness of the etheric substance is necessary before a man can be aware of anything but the physical world. It comes to some adults because of shock or strain or it may be a constant condition for the sensitive or clairvoyant. But for the majority the kingdom of childhood is closed by the time maturity is reached and the life of the senses has to suffice until death sets them free.'

Andrew took up the subject at this point:

'I can carry that account of the development of the child a little further,' he said. 'You have spoken of the building up of the etheric form in advance of the physical and its anticipation of the growth to be followed by the body. The astral, meanwhile, has gathered in nebulous fashion around the tiny child and he begins to use this medium directly. The ego attracts it to a centre around which it may gather but has as yet no control over it. There is thus an immense task before the ego. It has to weld together all these powers and to learn all over again how to manifest itself in matter.

'For the ego has returned, not only from different conditions, but from far distant times and it has to master its world all over again, as well as to regain control over a physical body. So the ego-being, which is best thought of as a personality pattern, takes possession of the developing embryo and begins to mould together its physical, etheric and astral substances. As you have said, the etheric anticipates the physical and these two grow together in close co-operation. The astral, meanwhile, is unformed but powerful and it is only by slow degrees that the child learns to use and control it. Thus the ego rebuilds its tenement and the physical heredity of the body modifies the ego.'

'How I wish that I had realised this mode of development sooner,' I said. 'It throws light on so many of the difficulties one encounters in the training of children. But how afraid it makes one of the delicate and intricate business of handling a child! In some respects children are so much nearer to reality than grown-ups and in others they need so much help, largely because of this lack of control over their emotional natures. Their desires and impulses are so much too strong for them.'

'Yes, mothers should be clairvoyant and to do them

162

justice I think they often are,' said Andrew. 'You see,' he went on, 'no child comes to a family haphazard. It has a strong connection with that particular group of people, or perhaps only with some one member of it and the task has been laid upon it to work out in that new setting some problem that it failed to solve in a previous life.'

'That throws a helpful light on family relationships,' I said. 'Some members of a family appear to mean so little to one and others are vitally important. Also, at certain stages of life one member will suddenly become very significant and others will fade into the background.'

'Yes,' said Andrew. 'The significance of any relationship within a family has its roots in a past which is inaccessible at that time. I wonder whether we should be more successful in working out these old problems if we were fully aware of what lies behind them? Probably not; for we are spared the knowledge of past failures and so have a fresh start in mastering them this time. I am speculating about this little group of ours. We have worked together for a long time now in close sympathy and understanding. I wonder how we shall arrange ourselves next time?'

I caught a chuckle from Scott.

'I'm beginning to look forward to next time. "What larks" as Joe Gargery put it.'

Here Scott transmitted such a comical picture of a succession of absurd possibilities in which we all filled incongruous roles that we finished with a hearty laugh. He had a unique power of presenting a series of mental pictures with flashing clearness and of showing himself as actively engaged therein in all manner of rapid and energetic caricatures. This particularly absurd series put an end to serious work for the moment.

*　　*　　*

163

I had been very interested by the accounts E.K. and Andrew had given us of the re-entry of the ego into the embryo. To theorise about such an event was one thing, but to have a practical picture of it was another. Inevitably, Wordsworth's rendering of the return in the famous Ode, came to mind. From the boundless ocean of universal life, back into the restraints and limitations of our life here,

Not in entire forgetfulness, and not in utter nakedness,
But trailing clouds of glory do we come,
From heaven, which is our home.

All mothers, I thought, have a dim understanding of this as they tend the tiny child. Something beyond the beauty of earth is sensed in the pure and innocent joy of being that shines out from the eyes of the infant. Poets know it, too. I thought of Blake's *Infant Joy*

'I have no name:
I am but two days old.'
What shall I call thee?
'I happy am,
Joy is my name.'
Sweet joy befall thee!

Francis Thompson gives us the same haunting impression of the poignant innocence and purity of childhood in his lovely picture of the child Jesus:

And did thy Mother let thee spoil
Thy robes, with playing on our soil?

But here Andrew broke in on my thoughts.

'I wonder,' he said, 'whether we could ever have been wise and loving enough for that responsibility if we had had the son for whom we both longed? The more I consider what is involved in parenthood, the more I marvel at this valiant, fearful gift of life. It is ruled by a necessity far beyond our conscious understanding, and yet it must govern our progress from age to age. We have to go on until we are purged of all evil, clear of all conflict, one with ourselves and at peace. We cannot stay until we have reached a state as near to the nature of pure love and joy as is possible to us; to become again as little children, in fact, and that purified state is our goal for each long cycle of being.

'How long we remain in this heavenly realm I do not know, but the ego-spirit becomes used to living in this atmosphere of pure being in which it breathes the very air of love and joy. Here is our home, here our native air, attained at last at the cost of who knows what of struggle, suffering and sinning, repenting, expiating and accepting. At last we are at home—in the Father's mansions, even if as yet, we may not come into His presence. I think I understand now what is the deep hunger and desire which assails us in all experiences of beauty. It is the nostalgia for home, for the never quite forgotten bliss we have had to leave. It is the pain of comparing the earthly with the unfading knowledge of the heavenly. I doubt whether the most evil, lost and wandering soul ever loses this hunger of desire, and sooner or later it must bring him back up the steep ascent and into the Fatherland.

'But the returning ego has to submit to exile and to exchange the world of pure love for the struggling life of the flesh. What wonder that it brings back with it a deep need for this same atmosphere of love? The satisfaction of this need is as vital to the newly born infant as the elementary food with which its body is nourished. For now, alas, the ego is no longer living freely in an air of love; it has to learn to live penuriously in a world where it breathes every kind of emotion, good and bad, poisonous as well as lifegiving. From this environment it can draw only a grudging scarcity of love. With what eagerness the child turns to the smile of love, how it suns itself in that influence and how it thrives while it can get sufficient of this vital food for the health of the astral body! Thus the child's first need is to find and attach itself to some source of love upon which it can feed. It quests its environment for this as strongly as it strives for its mother's milk.

'The ego has also to learn the difficult art of inter-action with the physical in its own body, as well as in its environment. Even to us, matter appears as the most dull and heavy stuff, and to the ego-spirit its inert and hopeless mass, stubborn and intractible, must fill the soul with a sense of helplessness in which I see the source of the deeply seated fear which no human being escapes. There below all that is conscious is this abyss of fear and arising from it are most of the states we term "evil". As the ego seeks to work its will upon the environment so it meets at every turn the inert resistance of matter. The organism reacts against this and so avoids the paralysis of the original dread and helplessness, but when the will to resist is tainted with fear, anger is produced. The outgoing being, meeting with opposition is thrown back upon itself and in the nega-tion of that recoil the conflicting emotional power turns to anger. The blow produces the spark; in the spark of anger some part of the being burns and dies and the morti-fied emotion returns to the self, which projects it outward in a harmful wave.

'Now the child meets with frustration at every turn. Physically, matter is too heavy and strong for him and his helplessness is an ever present realisation. His will, which is the ego in control, is constantly being frustrated even by those he loves and so fear and anger are continually being packed away into his unconscious mind. Add to these things the universal hunger and greed for far more love than can be got out of the child's human environ-ment and you have the basic ingredients of suffering and evil.

'Fear, of course, is at the bottom of the secondary evils of selfishness, self-assertion and aggressiveness; in fact, it looks as though fear is the parent of all human evil. Anger and hate are forms of the same negative emotions and cruelty is a sorrowful mixture of craving for love, attraction and repulsion and anger. It is easy to see, too, that the lust for power springs directly from an early sense of insecurity and that it is strongly developed in proportion to that insecurity. One sees the cure for all these things in the love and security which the returning ego should be able to demand as its right. If a child could be embodied who is satisfied and safe in both these respects, evil would no longer be worked into the unconscious levels of the astral body, to vitiate the conscious life through all its later experience.'

Scott said:

'I want to add to that. I believe that this struggle is the maker of form. The patterns of behaviour which make up the richness and worth of a personality could be set in no other way than as reactions to the series of frustrations which bewilder the ego at every turn. If there were no frustrations it might remain beautiful and pure, but it would be unformed, characterless and to my mind, far less valuable. It is surely in these subtle, intricate and unique patternings of personality that our highest value lies. By reason of our fight against frustration we all create something new in the world of being, whereas without the frustrations we should tend to more conformity with an ideal but dull pattern. Not that this is an argument for evil living—far from it. Quite without man-made evils there is enough of struggle and difficulty in life in the mere conflict with the flesh and the inert matter of the environment. Nature sees to that. All the same, I give my voice to the goodness of the struggle, to the joy of overcoming difficulties and of wrestling for the mastery over both flesh and matter. It is all exceedingly worth while, because without it there would be no occasion for men to develop some of the finest qualities we know—courage, endurance and love of adventure.'

Chapter Twelve

'The idea of the ego-being returning into a human body and bringing with it the potential records of many past lives, throws an interesting light on modern theories of the unconscious mind,' I said to Andrew.

'Your psychologists must be hard put to it to account for all they find in the unconscious by invoking only the incidents of one lifetime,' Andrew replied.

'Yes,' I said. 'They come upon a level of buried experience which was laid down in infancy, but, deeper than this, their case-books record material of a very different nature, archaic and fantastic to a degree which is difficult to trace to any knowledge or experience of the present life. Jung cites cases where a man who is deranged makes use of a symbol or notion that is only to be found among the mythological material of remote ages, among records of Ancient Egypt or perhaps Chaldea or India; he is convinced that his patient can have no previous conscious knowledge of such abstruse material. He is so impressed by this mysterious content of the unconscious that he has put forward a theory to account for it. He considers that it must be due to the transmission of race-history through heredity and that it resides in a part of the unconscious he calls "The Collective Unconscious" which it is supposed we share with all other men. How *experience* can be so transmitted remains a mystery, because nowadays the idea that acquired characteristics, let alone experiences, can be transmitted to descendants is scouted by biologists.'

'Hmm,' said Andrew. 'Most of the trouble, I think, comes

from the tendency to divide a man into "mind" and "body" —to cut him off at the neck, as it were and to think of his head as leading a different kind of life from his trunk. It is no better when you try to imagine "mind" as existing outside the body and as working independently of it. Then your monist comes along and dismisses all that as dualism and has, himself, to fall back on an explanation which makes mind the mere mechanical result of body-processes. And so you go on to one absurdity from another.

'Our analysis into physical-etheric-astral-ego substances does away with this attempt to split a man into body and mind and substitutes for it the conception of a fourfold body in which the whole man is involved in every activity, be it mental or physical. He can be active at many different levels according to which of his fourfold bodies is chiefly engaged. Each of these interpenetrating forms is geared-in to the others and no one of them can act in isolation from the rest. The conscious mind selects its own mode of experiencing and can be occupied mainly with the physical, or with the etheric or with the astral; it can even stand off from them all and regard its own ego-activity. When the ego is directed on to the etheric-physical level it is concerned mainly with bodily sensations, but it cannot avoid a modification of the astral and ego bodies in consequence of its attention to a lower level. For instance, when you suddenly hurt yourself you attend chiefly to your physical-etheric sensation of pain but there may also be an emotional reaction of distress or anger and an ego-reaction by which you realise how you have come to hurt yourself and how to avoid doing so in future.

'When you are concerned with desires and feelings the astral body is the centre of activity but there will be definite reactions in the physical-etheric bodies and the ego will be dealing with the significance of your feelings at the same time. Even when you are at work on the highest levels of thought, imagination and intuition, energy will be withdrawn from all the other bodies to sustain the effort. Where hard intellectual work has to be done the astral body is often drained of power by the demand for the sustaining of *interest* which is the emotional side of the task and it will be quite exhausted after the effort.

'This view of the fourfold being covers the whole range of physical and mortal activities without any straining of the evidence. There is no further mystery about the much-discussed mind-body relation, nor any need of the elaborate theories to which the problem has given rise. The brain, which concentrates all experience, is fourfold also and functions on each level, so it does not need to be regarded as a separate entity. It is the servant of each and all. Once one gets rid of the mind-body distinction all human experience is seen as the whole body at work on one or another of its energy levels. When it comes to the highest of these levels, the ego-activity, I admit that here is an energy which is invisible and formless but I believe it may be a visible substance on its own plane of being, nevertheless.

'The human being, then, is an organism which can be active on four levels of experience yet no activity can be isolated on one level.

'I have been thinking of it as a four-storey house,' I said, 'and the ego as the tenant who can occupy which floor he wishes.'

'That is not a good analogy,' said Andrew, 'because activity cannot be confined to any one floor. If the self is moving about in the attic, for instance, the furniture on the second and first floors will move in sympathy and even the basement will feel the disturbance. No, the house analogy won't do because the division between the levels of experience is not complete. The ego may identify itself for the time being with one or the other of its levels of experience, but since all are interconnected, all must reflect the activity in their respective medium.

'But now we want to relate this fourfold activity to the unconscious mind. Let me try to sum up the view taken by psychology. Unconscious mind is usually taken to be the emotion-charged but repressed memories which are unable to make their way into consciousness and so cause a state of ferment below the conscious level. They seek all the time to make their way into consciousness, to escape the censor, and to realise themselves in action and they affect conscious behaviour indirectly but powerfully whenever they can find such an outlet. This dangerous hidden matter succeeds in finding vent whenever we allow ourselves to be swayed by an impulsion which is not controlled by reason. We should suspect such an escape whenever we get passionate over a cause which is not in itself important enough to justify our heat. In cases of neuroses or insanity it is concluded that the unconscious mind has succeeded in gaining the upper hand in spite of the higher controls of reason and consciousness and has become free to work out its highly charged and often dangerous contents.'

'Is this a fair summary of the psychological view?' said Andrew.

'Yes, I think so. The emphasis is put mainly upon the repression and perversion of sex instincts as a rule, though Adler thinks the power impulses more important and Jung takes a more general view and puts at least some of the blame on the Collective, or Race-unconscious.'

'There is no need to limit the trouble to any one of the emotional impulses,' said Andrew. 'The whole emotional nature is involved in this study of the unconscious mind and it may exhibit its activity in any kind of impulse or desire. But to get at this problem we must be quite clear what we understand by memory. You can't define memory although you begin to discover many things about the way it works. There are several difficult and contradictory theories, all depending on the fallacious mind-body distinction, which is the greatest hindrance to clear thinking in psychology.

'The power to recall the past is due to the lighting up of the records made in all the body substances. Each body substance makes and keeps an inviolate record of every activity it has ever known. Each experience in a lifetime has set its own vibratory system going in the substances of physical, etheric and astral forms and these vibrations endure as long as the substances in which they act. This is a perfectly reasonable thing if you think of the nature of these substances. In themselves they are simply systems of activity and that activity is modified permanently by every phase of existence. For instance, the matter of your four brain-substances will never be quite the same after you have grasped this idea. The set of vibrations corresponding to that piece of knowledge will be there until you die, and after if they are also imprinted on the astral substance.

'Now what happens when you remember? Your ego consciousness selects and lights up certain vibrations in the physical-etheric-astral bodies. They have been there all the time but you have not been attending to them; you have "forgotten" them. Now the peculiar quality of earth memory depends on the interreflection between all three records and where the experience has been recorded by all three the recollection is complete and the forgotten experience comes fully back into consciousness with every detail clear and accurate. But sometimes only one or two principles of your being have taken part in the experience, as when you have performed some action without full attention because your thought (astral-ego) was elsewhere. Then the record is incomplete in one or more mediums and the ego will find it very difficult or even impossible to recall the experience.

'Childhood is a special case of this kind of partial experience. The physical and etheric are active from the beginning but the astral connection is fitful and the ego has as yet no control of the being. Many records will then be made in the child's astral, etheric-physical natures over which the ego will have no power since the records are partial and so impossible to recall. From the earliest infancy the imperishable records are being made in each body-substance; the physical records itself as body habits, the etheric as life habits, the astral as desire and emotional habits and yet none of these early records can be lit up by consciousness.

'After consciousness, that is, the ego-being, has been fully integrated with the other principles the emotional record is made for the most part above the level of consciousness and so is capable of recall by the memory, which is the ego in its backward-looking aspect. It is here, in these early buried memories, especially the emotional ones burnt into the astral substance that the psychologist looks for the origin of the unconscious mind. They are deep enough, and troublesome enough, these early memories, but they are emphatically not all that it contains.'

'It is known that very painful experiences have a tendency to sink below the level of recall for good, even when they have been experienced in full consciousness. How do you account for this?' I asked.

'Such experiences inflict painful and dangerous wounds in the actual stuff of the astral body. These wounds are difficult to heal and may cause disease or deformity as well as acute suffering. You would avoid touching a wound of this kind in your physical body and you would strenuously prevent anyone else doing so unless your reason took charge and made you realise that wounds must be attended to. Now the astral body is terribly sensitive. You will find out how keenly it experiences everything when you have no longer a physical form to dull its reactions. Moreover, the astral is very little under the control of reason—far less so than you like to imagine. Reason is more often its slave than its master. So when the astral sustains a deep and painful wound it desires to avoid any touch on that wound. The place where the painful vibrations are active becomes taboo; the ego may not light up that particular area since the negative urge is too strong for it to overcome. Hence such wounds and disablements may remain hidden to be a constant source of unconscious misery and difficulty during a lifetime. I am very familiar with this kind of trouble, because, although you may succeed in "forgetting" these things during life, the record is still in your astral body and when I, as a physician, examine your astral body because you are ill and in pain these old injuries have to be found and cured.

'You cure them yourself directly you stop running away from them and allow understanding and love to control your reaction to the original injury. They cannot be cured while you are reacting to them with resentment. That causes the festering of the wound which poisons your whole being. We can treat these injuries with certain emanations from our own bodies, but the patient has to co-operate in the cure.'

'So when our psychologists use methods of association or even hypnosis to force the injury into consciousness and to get the patient to look at it squarely and accept it, they are going the right way to work?' I asked.

'Entirely the right way; and if they succeed in healing trauma we should be most grateful to them, since otherwise the cure has to be postponed for us to deal with after death.'

175

'I have just one thing to add to that,' said Andrew. 'Many astral injuries heal automatically. Even serious injuries would do that if they were not made permanent by resentment. I meant quite literally what I said about the festering of astral wounds. That is due to resentment and bitterness and no wound will heal while its condition is thus kept septic. It is quite right and proper to forget injuries once the wounds they have caused have healed but that is a different thing from forcing them below the level of consciousness by anger and fear. If this is done they go deep below the level of accessibility and remain permanently in a dangerously poisonous condition. You can imagine the suffering they cause after death when the astral consciousness is filled with the pain they are causing.'

'Forgiving one's enemies becomes a highly practical piece of clinical advice, then, and not just a high moral precept one cannot be expected to take seriously,' I said.

'I never cease to remind you that the teaching of Christ has that immediate and necessary connection with health and well being as we see them here. I wish it was more obvious to you on earth,' said Andrew.

'Now if you are quite clear about the structure of the fourfold body, and the work done by each of its elements, we will go on to enquire what the ego brings into its new life,' said Andrew.

'To understand this we must trace the course of events following upon physical death. The physical body remains on earth and the etheric is shed soon after, as you know. Both these bodies have been instruments of the personality and have added in their own way to its meaning. The possession of a beautiful body, for instance, builds into the emotions and ego a certain type of feeling and thought; a healthy etheric body adds an intensity of energy, and so the essential meaning of the discarded bodies becomes a part of the astral-ego make-up. So, although the material aspect of these bodies has been lost their essential meaning is carried on into the new life.'

'Please go slowly. I am trying to connect this with the permanent systems of vibration set going by experience,' I said.

'Good,' said Andrew. 'There you have the material aspect. Those vibratory systems, reflected from the other bodies are still part of the astral-ego. They can only be recorded in those bodies in the form of feeling and thought so that is the permanent memory meaning as it exists now. For instance, if your physical body has suffered injury and your etheric body the consequent pain, when the event is recalled you can only re-experience the emotions you felt, such as fear or resentment—and the thought which accompanied it. These are the astral-ego reactions and they are the only kind of memory you now have.

'If that is clear, let us follow the process a little further. Our bodies are now reduced to these two elements, astral and ego, the feeling and thinking bodies. The astral is usually undeveloped at first, often diseased and seldom fully under ego control. The next process, that of the maturing and discarding of the astral will therefore be delayed until maturity is reached. So the era of our existence on the astral planes is usually the longest term of the whole cycle. It seems to me that the purifying and perfecting of the emotional body is our main task here. Eventually, when this is completed, the astral substance will be cleansed and cured, the body well formed and controlled by the ego and the man as astral being will enjoy a supremely happy maturity. This, after a longer or shorter time, will pass into a gradual decay, or rather, gradual transformation into the next order of being. Then the mature and beautiful astral body will be left behind but before this flaming robe of the spirit is finally laid aside it will have passed on to the ego the essence and meaning of its whole long existence with all the poignant variety of its emotional experiences throughout this cycle of living. The ego will retain it as essential meaning, but more than that it will retain the special power of intuition, which is the *feeling*—form of thought, an activity which has been established by the co-operation of astral and ego modes of being. As they have worked together to establish this power so now the ego can exercise it alone in a purer and keener form than ever. So the sum of the whole personality will now include the up-gathered meaning of every phase and mode of its long existence.

'I have reached the stage when the purgation of my earth-life is practically finished and now I am beginning to recall and understand the lives that I have lived before. These ancient records have been buried in *my* unconscious for long enough, but the ego could not begin to deliver up its deeper secrets until I had finished with my past life and had reached a stage when consciousness could illumine them. Now, whenever I am free from actual work or affairs my mind goes back in time and impressions of the far-off days of other lives come slowly into focus, change and dissolve into others, so that by degrees I am becoming familiar with its setting and events.

'These processes take varying times with different people. I must have spent about five hundred years here before I came back to earth in 1890 and I should be glad if I might have as long a sojourn here again. For some people it is longer, of course. It is possible to take two thousand years to reach the final stage of ego simplicity. As yet I do not quite understand the mysterious necessity that brings the spirit back again to earth, but I am satisfied that when it comes it will be because this cycle of being has reached a just and natural conclusion.'

Here Andrew ceased.

I was glad to be able to relate the theory of the fourfold body to the known principles of heredity. That these operate we know, but that they are a sufficient explanation of the whole human inheritance has always been uncertain. The transmission of physical features by way of a long line of ancestry obviously governs the type of body and this must limit the self-expression of the returning ego. In effect, every man has a double heredity; through a long line of physical ancestry and also through a long line of ego incarnations. Each rebirth allows a modification of an age-old personality pattern because of its modification by the legacy of a physical body.

But with every rebirth the ego must bring back added meaning and richness in its personality pattern and so it will have ever more power to mould its material body into a fitting expression for the spirit. The element of novelty in each rebirth is wonderfully adapted to give the ego a chance of adding a new and better chapter to its long life-history, yet the unique personality remains the same in succeeding lives, only enriching itself by each new cycle of experience. So the ego returns into a new body, conditioned by a new environment, to try conclusions again with a new earthly fate.

Later on, Andrew returned to the same subject:

'It has taken aeons of time to produce this fourfold body of man. The evolutionary evidence can be read in the development of the human body but that is only the physical side of the story. The study of doubtfully human remains tells us less than the study of embryology. The ego, in its character of the potentiality for human life, brings back with it the stored up meaning of the whole series of recurring lives and it begins to modify the developing embryo so that it recapitulates the early stages of the series. The scroll of evolutionary time is unrolled from the beginning going through the scale of animal forms until in nine months it has repeated them up to the emergence of the human form itself. Birth marks the point where the unwinding scroll reaches the authentic human form, but this is not the end of the scroll since the ego may have had many descents to earth since it first took on the form of a man and these too must be recapitulated before maturity is reached. They also are recorded in the ego and after birth their turn comes to influence the new life.'

'Psychologists and educators have paid some attention to the recapitulation process in children. There has been an attempt to link it with Jung's Collective Unconscious,' I said. 'There is no doubt that children pass through easily recognisable stages which seem to reflect the history of the race.'

'We see it as the repetition of each individual's previous earth lives and as a direct continuation of the ego-tendency to act over again its past incarnations.'

'That really simplifies the problem,' I said, 'for Jung's theory presents difficulties as to the manner of their inheritance. I am certain from my own observation that the growing child does pass through well-defined periods of behaviour, phases after which his attitude to life alters as another phase succeeds. These changes affect his speech, his play and his dreams. They pass and are discarded at the right time if they are allowed scope to express themselves fully. This last is important, since if they are too severely checked there may occur what is known as an "infantile fixation". Development is then held up at this stage and the child attitude may be carried on into the life of the adult, often with regrettable results.'

'Here, then, is our evidence reappearing after birth,' said Andrew. 'The child, in its play, its day dreams and fantasies and also in its dreams is living out the stored meaning of each lifetime since he reached the status of man. I think this process has to be fully played out before the entire energy of the youth can be directed into the experiences of his present life. When he does turn freely to the present we have the beginning of maturity. If this recapitulation has been well done these buried lives can sleep happily in the unconscious and they will not transmit old fears to the present mind of the child. Joy and triumph as well as fears and sorrows will be acted out in play in the new environment. Old fears will be seen to be groundless and so will be dissipated. But if they cannot thus be released in play it is easy to see that they may remain active in the unconscious to mar the present experience.'

'One cannot miss certain obvious recapitulations,' I said, 'such as the fear of darkness, the phase of animal fears when it becomes a fearful joy to play at lions and tigers and so turn a real fear into a harmless fantasy which need no longer be taken seriously.'

'Yes, no doubt one could build up a whole series of these recapitulations in order of their usual appearance in the child's mind, although there will be many variations since no two people will have lived the same life, even if they have shared the same primitive conditions. The important thing is that many unconscious records fraught with the possibility of real suffering are played out in harmless make-believe by the child who can release them without understanding their significance. This is a harmless catharsis of old fears and angers which might otherwise paralyse mature life.'

'Typical play activities, both social and solitary, would make a fascinating study from this angle,' I said.

'Undoubtedly. For the full record of previous lives, study the child's recapitulations. Sometimes this dangerous material finds outlet in the child's dreams and explains their terrifying nature. Any child may be loaded up with perilous stuff relating to some disastrous experience in a past life and it is for parents to be patient with the queer and often inconvenient behaviour which this may induce. The solution is to give unrestricted expression to the fantasies and play activities of children, guiding and restraining them only when they are definitely anti-social or harmful.

'Another thing became clear to me when I reached the retrospect of my own childhood days. One finishes with the part of one's life which was always open to consciousness and then the early part of childhood with its peculiarly keen but very chaotic emotional record comes back into experience again. In fact, the Freudian unconscious is now accessible. Here I made an impressive discovery and one that illustrates still more clearly the necessity for dealing easily with children. I found that the emotional reactions of those early days—reactions which had never reached consciousness in the ordinary sense—were enormously strong; in fact, the biggest storms of later life pale into feebleness before the intensity of the emotions felt by the very young child. Apparently the impact of emotion before it is under any sort of control by the ego is a fearful thing. There is astonishing pain felt, keen sense of frustration, acute jealousy and a perfect anguish of desire.

'I want you to pause and try to realise the battle which has to be fought by the infant in its struggle for love

182

and significance and in its reactions against new fears and insecurity. I passed as a happy, contented sort of child, I believe, but there was a most astonishing volcano of emotion erupting in me most of the time. I conclude that the only way to balance all this is to be able to satisfy the child's hunger for love and craving for security. We must cease to be so casual in our treatment of children.'

Andrew next suggested that the series of recurring life-times which had gone to the making of a man of our own times could be shown in diagrammatic form. He said:

'Build up a diagram that will show the conscious and unconscious levels of mind in life after life, so that it shows clearly the gathering complexity of the unconscious levels as the ego returns continually to earth, adding each time another layer of potential experience. Begin with the stage when the organism is first a man. The unconscious levels then will hold only a record of animal experiences which will be fully recapitulated before birth. Go on in series from that showing how life piled on life has created this wonderful mind of modern man.'

The following diagram grew up in response to his demand. (Page 100, C.B.)

1st CYCLE CONSCIOUS LEVEL
UNCONSCIOUS LEVEL
STRATIFIED ANIMAL
EXPERIENCES

Then comes the second cycle which will give above the animal strata the first level of human experience from the preceding cycle (A and a).

2nd CYCLE CONSCIOUS LEVEL
UNCONSCIOUS LEVEL
LAST HUMAN LIFE
ANIMAL EXPERIENCES

Or, to put the thing straight away into series, it will go on like this:

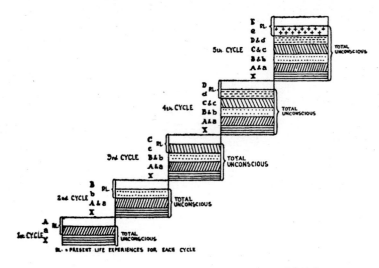

There are four lives in this series, and in the later ones the recurrence of AaBbCcDd are not actual memories but vague emotional records developed in the unconscious astral body.

Chapter Thirteen

Andrew began now to redeem his promise to tell me something about the panorama of the distant past which was beginning to unfold to his vision. Perhaps the intense interest I took in this was due to the presence of similar material hidden in my own unconscious mind, but as the story proceeded it gave me great satisfaction because it completed my knowledge of Andrew's life and character, explained anomalies in his conduct which had always been dark to me and showed me many hidden motives and meanings in his personality. I had known him intimately, or so I thought; we had grown up together and had shared interests and occupations for years. But, as with most of our friends on earth, there had always remained a sense of apartness and of the mystery which one human being must hold for another even in the closest relationship. I began to see that this unknown quantity we sense in each other may be due to the hidden history of the past—a past which perhaps we did not share with each other. Unknown and uncharted, this part of the personality will yet operate strangely and will provide the unexpected element in the relationship. It is, I suppose, this unshared past which gives us the conviction of ultimate aloneness, and as we cannot know in what this isolation consists we often allow it to sadden us. We say, 'How little we know even our nearest and dearest!' Intuitively we have grasped the fact that a great deal of the personality of our friends exists apart and cannot be shared because it is below consciousness. This is, perhaps, the first time that the two lives have run alongside and so only the recent level of the being can be shared.

On the other hand, there are men and women who are recognised immediately one meets them. Intuitive knowledge and confidence go deep and there is an instant sense of ease and safety in the contact which cannot be justified by our short experience of them on earth. There are no problems to work out in such relationships and no need to explain oneself. Communion is effortless and happy from the beginning. Nearly everyone has been fortunate enough to have such an experience but where such a contact ripens into a closer companionship one gets those rare associations which account for all the great love stories of the past. Andrew, no doubt, will tell me that these are people who have met and loved before and have worked out in a previous lifetime all their problems of mutual adjustment. They are united *below* the level of consciousness as well as above it and no hidden and unshared mystery can wreck their relationship.

But here is Andrew's next communication:

'I hope I made it plain last time that one explores all of the unconscious in this process of recollection. I left off when the record had reached the stormy and chaotic experiences of early childhood. Sometime after this had passed I began to get glimpses of a more distant range of events; different men, different manners and different scenes were recognised in a dimmer, but still definite way. I found that one does not see oneself moving objectively in these scenes; one is there, feeling and moving in the strange environment but one's personal consciousness is not quite the same. There is a subtle difference in the outlook and sympathies which is hard to define. One is acting in the past scene, but yet is conscious of the more developed present personality. The self thus appears in a different guise and one has to recognise that in those days one had habits and modes of thought and behaviour which were strange and uncouth even if not completely alien to the mind of the man of the present.

'I have known men who are badly broken by this experience of their past. They may have lived good and respectable lives in their latest incarnation and it is very hard for them to face themselves in a more crude and brutal phase of their long existence. One of the most startling things that may have to be faced is a change of sex, though this is not an invariable experience. I leave to your imagination the extraordinary self-revelations which may have to be accepted but there is no doubt that in this hidden material we come on the ultimate clues to one's attitude to life and the queer contradictions in conduct which do not seem to fit into the pattern. Luckily, these older recollections are not charged with emotion as are the ones that have gone before; they are more dreamlike and yet at the same time more charged with meaning, and this is because they come out of the ego-memory and are no longer involved with an astral memory. Hence they are in terms of meaning and have lost the pull of the emotional element. Another thing needs to be realised: where guilty and shameful deeds have to be acknowledged in one's past life, one experiences them from the *inside*, so to speak, and not as they might be seen by an observer. One reads of deeds of horror in history but the narrator can only guess at the motives. When one re-experiences the events, one finds that one's motive was hardly ever completely bad and luckily, one realises only the meaning of the act as it was viewed by the self and not as it was judged by others.'

'This retrospect must be so fascinating that I wonder how you can keep track of the present in which you are living with such strange pictures of the past occupying your mind,' I said.

'My ordinary life goes on as usual,' said Andrew. 'This is my thought life, my subjective experience. It may sound bewildering but it is not so in practice. I agree that it is a fascinating study as you can guess, but you have not yet realised the importance of the process.

'By thus taking possession of more and more of myself I am becoming a more complete individual. As I reclaim the unconscious part of my being the area of my personality is increased and I become possessed of more strength and power of being. When I have explored and accepted the whole of my past I shall be a complete man, since the strength hitherto locked up in my unconscious self will at last be released for conscious use.'

'I see,' I said. 'That is Jung's dream of the perfect man, the complete, integrated man, and yet he realises that it is nearly impossible to achieve such control over the unconscious while on earth. I suppose that when you have gathered in the power from the farthest reach of your personality you will be a very formidable person.'

'We shall all go through the same process and those who have had the longest series of earth-lives and thus have the greatest store of meaning to reconquer, will command the greatest reserves of strength. I have only just begun to realise the last two of my earth lives as yet and there may be many more to unfold. Shall I tell you something about these two incarnations in case I can thus throw light upon the general problem?'

'Please do, Andrew. That is just what I want,' I said.

'I have twice been born an Englishman,' Andrew went on, 'once, late in the nineteenth century, as you know, and previous to that about half-way through the fifteenth century, so there has been a comparatively short interval be-

188

tween these two lives; less than five hundred years, in fact. When I first began to recall this fifteenth-century life I got visions of myself in a setting of warfare but now the bow was used instead of the rifle and mounted men-at-arms ranged a countryside that was familiar to me. It was France, but the France of an earlier and cruder age. I was an English soldier fighting in France again and we had a peculiar fear of our enemy whom we thought in league with the devil. Certainly they routed us in battle and out-manoeuvred us in the field. Yet for me personally, it was an active and not unhappy life with very much the same feeling about it as this last. I was cheerful with my fellows, fairly popular and only unhappy about a woman in England to whom I had behaved badly even by my stand-ards of that life. Well, it was a very short life and it ended in the same way and at about the same age and again on a battle field in France.

'I have thought a lot about this queer recurrence of the same theme in both lives and am pretty sure there is nothing accidental about it. At first I thought that the repetition of the same motif—patriotism urging me to a military life and a short, stirring adventure of campaigning on foreign soil must be due to some quality of my ego which found its best fulfilment in that particular pattern of life; I was prepared to find it repeated again in the preced-ing set of memories but now I see that there is more in it than that. For, putting together the two lives of which we have spoken I come upon corroboration of the theory of recapitulation. You remember that up to the age of twenty-one I was a most pacifically minded young man and that all my feelings were strongly anti-military?'

'Yes,' I said. 'That is how I remember you best.'

'Then, for no very obvious reason I suddenly took it into my head to join a Territorial Unit. I gave myself

189

excellent reasons for this such as need of physical training, male companionship and so on, but the urge was probably quite independent of these careful arguments.'

'Why, yes,' I said. 'I had known you a long time and had never associated that kind of interest with you at all. Then you suddenly sprang this decision on us and I at least was always puzzled by it. But I had so much admiration for you that you could do no wrong so I don't suppose you realised my surprise and consternation.'

'Yes, but don't you see? That was where my last life overtook me. I had been a soldier then and the same urge repeated its special theme just as I reached manhood. In peacetime it would have worked out harmlessly enough but in 1913 it linked me up with the military machine just in time so that when war broke out in 1914 I was a partly trained man and was at once swept into the fighting. But for the change in my outlook which so suddenly took away my distaste for the life of a soldier I doubt if I should have enlisted at all. I might have waited to be conscripted and so have survived the war. That was Karma in operation with a vengeance: my past life modifying the present one and coming into play just at the right moment to bring about a similar pattern. I am convinced that re-capitulation is a powerful instrument of Karma in producing a recurring theme in life after life.

'For, you see, that urge from my fifteenth-century life did not appear until I had nearly reached maturity so it is evident that recapitulation does not finish at adolescence but continues until one is really mature. Probably the crisis produced by that last intrusion of the past into the present is the sign that maturity has been reached and that the ego from then on will be free to devote its full energies to the present business of living. It means also that the last life as the final stage of recapitulation has the most effect in setting the governing theme of the present life. It also explains the experimental nature of the youth's attitude to life and his difficulty in choosing a career until he is finally free from the influences of his past lives.'

'If that last life is the influence that came into your life at twenty-one, I want to know the kind of life that influenced it before that time. Can you tell me something about the life that preceded the fifteenth-century one?' I asked.

'I have no means of deciding how long back this other life may have been. I can only tell you that the setting is that of ancient Rome and that the "I" who is central to it is a slave, and a woman at that. I appear to have lived and died in this condition and there seems no doubt that I was happy and well used in spite of my status. But this far-off life is only just beginning to reveal itself and it would be better to wait until the whole story has come into view before I enlarge upon it. I can select from what I have seen, however. Here is a very suggestive sketch of a family group.

'You will see in this the working of Karma in relation to a group as well as to individuals. Think of the group first in its modern form. It consists of a middle-class English family in which the mother is the dominating influence. She is a vigorous, sturdy woman with the head and brow of a man and a shrewd, yet urbane habit of thought. Her indomitable will and her organising power make her the undoubted head of the family. She is stern, conventional, yet kindly and strongly religious. There are four sons, the eldest of whom struggles free from his mother's control at an early age and is able to make his own pattern of life in spite of her influence. But between the second son and the mother there is a specially strong tie and he remains largely under her influence right up to manhood, and, indeed, until his early death in war. The third son conforms even more closely to his mother's wishes, but the youngest son, an attractive, charming child, so pretty that he is often taken for a girl, is not nearly so tractable. He is the particular pet and plaything of the second son, who "mothers" the boy right through his childhood, often shielding him from the stern punishments meted out by the mother; he is actually known as "Mick's baby", and only once does his champion fail him. This boy loathes study and will not learn. He finally runs away from home in weariness and disgust. He is brought back, of course, and on this occasion even Mick cannot condone his behaviour. The great war claims two victims from this family, the second son, and this youngest one.

'Now we return to the second son, who has reached the after-death stage when his distant past is coming into focus. He finds himself back in Roman times and the family group with which he is now associated contains familiar figures, but each filling very different roles. It is easy to recognise the modern mother in the form of a stern, stoic Roman citizen of strong passions and affections. He has a slave wife whom he loves devotedly, and a mother with whom he has strong ties of affection. But now, the erstwhile son has to recognise himself as the slave wife and he finds again the well loved younger brother as his own adored little daughter. The mother of the Roman citizen has been drawn back into relation with her son, and is the eldest child in the modern family. His tolerant affection for his mother and the ease with which he escapes her control in the later life is thus explained. The pull of affinity would seem to have been exerted by the Roman father, re-born as the mother of the modern family, and it has brought back to him, first, his mother's spirit as the eldest son, then his wife as second son, while the latter has drawn back into relationship with himself the little daughter. All that follows in the family history of the modern group is foreshadowed by their relation to each other in the past.'

'I do not know whether to laugh or cry over that, Andrew. I will not pretend that I do not recognise the picture, but the significance of the personalities as I knew them is so enlarged and re-interpreted by their past roles that it is strangely affecting. In fact, I am a little overwhelmed by the light it throws on what I naturally took to be a normal family group.'

'That is the effect one would expect from a sudden accentuation of the *meaning* of things and people. It is the kind of mental enlargement we constantly experience. You see, as everything deepens in meaningfulness one's own life is deepened and enlarged as well. It is a glimpse of the fulness of life of which we so often tell you.

'But here is another group study. There were once two brothers who were not good friends. All their earthly lifetime they were in conflict. When the time came to die, each gladly went his own way but in spite of themselves they could not avoid meeting here. Then they became able to see the truth about their discord; they found that in a previous life they had been the wives of one man and had been bitterly jealous of each other. Finding the meaning of their quarrel, they understood and were reconciled and in due course went back to earth again. The old attraction drew them into the same family but this time they were born as brother and sister. In this relation there was legitimate scope for the mingled attraction and opposition of their Karma and so in this last lifetime they could act and feel freely towards each other and yet clear themselves of the transgression which had hitherto spoilt their association. In this case there is seen the clearing of a difficult connection which had gathered guilt and reproach because of the continual failure to adjust. But when the relationship is perfected, when the two protagonists are finally cleared of guilt in respect of each other then the cord of Karma can be loosened and each may go free of the other if he so desires.

'I should like to give you many more instances of the way in which Karma works for the redemption of the soul from wrong and evil relations to one's fellows, but perhaps enough has been said to show that the process is an intensely meaningful one and that it plays a large part in the overcoming of evil in each individual life.'

'Then you think that we have to go on until everyone of our relationships are perfected and there is no longer any sense of guilt associated with them? That is a stern gospel. I suppose it means, too, that every time we set a wrong process at work we are making a chain to draw ourselves back into that association again and shall have to face it afresh in another form next time,' I said.

'Yes. We have to teach ourselves to regard our "lifetime" as this whole chain of existences, each of which is a mere incident in the total life for which we are responsible. Karma is really only the continuous meaning and purpose which binds together these incidents and makes them into an integrated whole.'

'I am glad that it is not necessary for me to face the whole story of my past yet; I am not adequate to such a prospect. I suspect,' I said, 'that it needs the larger scope of consciousness and the purer, finer quality of life which you have reached before it can be seen justly, or with equanimity. But I am almost oppressed by this vision of the intensely meaningful quality of living. Although I realise that in the long run this will bring a deeper power of experience, the serious import of this long view of our existences, linked and controlled by a slowly fulfilling purpose, fills me with the deepest awe. Blind mischances, broken hopes, loose ends of unsatisfactory relationships need no longer vex our souls as we come to die. They will recur and fit into a succeeding part of the pattern and we need no longer be haunted by the cry of "too late". There will always be time for our failures and our crimes to be expiated. The meaning of repentance is enhanced, because sincere contrition will permanently modify our being. It will give us the best chance of avoiding the same temptation next time and of making the reparation which perhaps this lifetime may deny us.'

Chapter Fourteen

There were many questions arising out of the application of the theory of re-birth and when next E.K. was with me we began to discuss them.

I said:

'I am not mathematical but surely the numerical aspect of our theory needs consideration. If there can be no human birth unless there is a returning ego to co-operate with the embryo how are we to account for a steadily increasing world population?'

'I have been considering that point,' said E.K., 'and I can see several factors which may come into play. First, consider the facts as they can be known on earth. Primitive populations were subject to great natural catastrophes—earthquakes, floods, glacial ages, submergences of land and so on. We have no means of knowing how numerous men were in those days but under primitive conditions it is likely that very few of the children born would be reared. A high death rate means a small earth population balanced by a correspondingly large number of souls in the after-death condition. These multitudes would seek rebirth again and again and if conditions were bad they might as often fail to survive childhood. So the variations in earth population must always have been balanced by the numbers here; more here, less on earth and the reverse. I think that the sum total of living souls has remained much the same throughout the ages but that life, like any other form of energy, changes its form and is now on the earth side, and now on our side of death.

'There are several other sources of returning life which may have flowed into the earth stream and may help to account for the increasing populations. The Atlantis legend, which supposes a highly-developed race existing for many generations on an extensive continent which has since been submerged, is almost certainly based on fact. In that great population of an earlier age was a storehouse of human material all of which must have reincarnated during succeeding ages. By degrees, all these advanced types of humanity must have been re-absorbed into the ebb and flow of life on earth and on the earth planes. Then I also firmly believe that there are other sources of life which can, on occasion transfer to our earth stream. The other planets of our system do not appear to support life in the earth sense, but they are certainly inhabited by spiritual beings who have as a rule, no need to incarnate in an earthly body. Life on earth is absorbingly interesting to other spiritual beings. They influence it, guide its main developments and sometimes make the supreme sacrifice of coming down into its darker mode of being themselves so as to influence it more directly. There may well be a small but steady addition to human numbers from these spheres. Many of the great spiritual leaders of mankind have thus originated.'

'Thank you, E.K. That does ease the problem. Nowadays it is also conceded that there may be inhabited planets in other solar systems and that would open still more possibilities of exchange, I suppose. But now, here is another question. What about murdered races, such for instance, as the Tasmanian, and what about extinct or dying breeds like the Amerindian or the Australian Aborigines?'

'You are realising that these souls can hardly come back to their own races and are wondering what happens to them when they need to come back to earth?'

'Yes,' I said. 'Whatever causes races to die out, the rebirth situation amounts to that. How can they come back to earth if their own race fails to provide them with physical bodies?'

'You can take it that they do return when the time comes and that, in the case of a primitive race, the time interval may be only a short one. I like to think that for the Tasmanians, where a whole race were callously exterminated, it is ironically just that they should be reborn into the race of their conquerors and murderers and I have little doubt that this is indeed the case. There is, for primitive people particularly a strong pull back to the same environment so they are most likely to return to their ancestral land and there inhabit whatever physical forms they can find. If this is so, it looks like the most exact and meticulous justice and I thank God for giving me this glimpse of it,' said E.K.

'That's interesting,' I said. 'I remember that in speaking of the Red Indian, Jung notes a great many physical and psychological resemblances between the Red Indian and the modern American and Canadian types. He comments on the shape of the head, the lean face, tight lips and so on. Then he points out that the white man is inclined to approve the Red Indian virtues, and still more significant, to adopt his symbols which shows a deep connection in the unconscious. Jung relates these facts to his own theory of the collective unconscious and also explains these resemblances by the influence of place in producing and modifying types.'

'It is far more likely that the returning Indian spirit, unable to re-incarnate in his own dying race, tends to be reborn into the families of his conquerors. He has to return when the time comes and for many reasons he is most likely to do so in the country of his ancestors. So life

198

is not nearly so unjust as a purely earth view of cause and effect would suggest. There is a compensating factor at work for which I rejoice. If reincarnation were a generally accepted theory, these facts would be quoted as clinching arguments.'

'Do you think, then, that one usually returns to the same race and country?' I asked.

'Various considerations of affinity govern the return, as I have said. Probably one cannot easily bring back an advanced ego-spirit into a physical body born of an immature race, so there must be limits to the interchanges between race and country, but within those limits changes do occur. Europeans, who are only superficially separated into national groups often descend into another race. I have in mind several instances of men and women who have done so. The strong affinities with other races felt by some of us on earth are probably due to the fact that we have previously lived out a lifetime among the people we now instinctively know and admire.'

Scott, who had been attending closely to this discussion, now broke in:

'I should like to link up the rebirth theory with historical facts, but since the subject would be too vast if treated in detail we must consider it in a general way.

'Arising out of my earth activities is a great interest in archaeology, particularly as it affects theories of evolution. It is a mistake to despise myths and legends in this connection especially where the same symbolic notion reappears in many forms in different languages. There is a persistent legend that somewhere in the human story there occurred a great fault and carry-over in the direct course of our development. The sense of a fall, of the loss of a golden age, of the tragedy of lost Atlantis, all probably have the same root. I interpret it like this:

199

'A race of men, finely developed in form and culture were the outcome of a long period of evolutionary history ages before any of the rootstocks of our present races were established. They were physically beautiful and had a high degree of sensitive awareness though their consciousness had a quality of innocence which made them unaware of the distinction between good and evil as we understand them. Then some great natural catastrophe overtook this race, perhaps the submergence of a continent, perhaps some great upheaval of volcanic origin. The race was overwhelmed as in the legends of lost Atlantis. From this disaster there were few survivors, and these were scattered, solitary and unable to maintain themselves. Finally, they were forced to coalesce with a sub-human race just emerging from the anthropoid ape stem. By this intermixture the true human characteristics were diluted and almost lost, but ultimately they re-emerged and reasserted themselves in the semi-human races of today.

'The original human survivors suffered much humiliation in their intercourse with the lower race with whom they mingled. Their offspring bore the marks of the brute and had to carry the shame of it. The guilt and humiliation of this lowering of the type sank deeply into the consciousness of the ensuing race. I contend that man today shows all the typical reactions of the hybrid, the half-breed, which has lost the innocence of both the animal and the human breed from which it sprang.

'I am going to cite the theory of recapitulation of evolutionary history in each human lifetime in support of this reconstruction of the human story. The time of life where I see this dark part of our story reappearing is at adolescence. It is the end of the lovely stages of infancy the closing phase of which I believe may correspond to the period in which the earlier human race reached its full development. In our present race, the pure and beautiful body of childhood has to give place to a maturity which is not nearly so beautiful and its innocence must be exchanged for a fuller self-consciousness accompanied by that queer balance of the mind we explain as the knowledge of good and evil.

'At this point I see the recapitulation of the experiences of the shamed and humiliated child-race of the past. A mixture of emotions certainly enters the experience of the growing child at this time which has no parallel among other animals and the physical changes that accompany puberty are often accompanied by the queer emotion of shame. Man alone has to endure this and I am pretty sure that it is not due merely to the arrival at fuller self-consciousness. In my view, it is an unnatural, unhealthy and dangerous emotion, quite out of line with any freely developing process of evolution which would never have produced such an odd reaction. In fact, at this period of life, if the recapitulation theory means anything at all, the yeasty emotional turmoil must indicate a period of history when there was a great emotional revolt against the animal processes of reproduction with all their attendant phenomena, and at the same time, on the physical side, a corresponding fascination and attraction as for a forbidden thing. A child who has no advance knowledge of the bodily changes due at this time is apt to be afraid and shocked as though what should be natural processes were so alien to his previous experience as to come with startling effect into his life. He has always to make a complicated and difficult adjustment to the new phase of life. Many of us never get over our distaste for the human body as though for some reason it was foreign to us. You may think this morbid, but I believe that most men are deeply dishonest in regard to their reactions to the human body and its functions.'

'That is a challenge,' said E.K. 'You are inferring that man has a different reaction to his own body from that of any other animal and that he has not troubled himself to find out why this should be so. Why does man take so much trouble to clothe his body, in fact? He does so for many secondary reasons, such as need for warmth, love of display and so on but these are certainly subordinate to his deep distrust and shame of his body. He tries hard nowadays to convince himself that he enjoys freedom from covering but his efforts never alter the behaviour of the majority of the race. I am inclined to agree that such an attitude is not in line with a natural development which would hardly cause such a funny kink in the mind as bodily shame because of the make-up of the human form. I find your idea very interesting. It certainly throws light on a queer human problem.'

'And here is another contribution to the thesis,' said Scott. 'The lost race had to reincarnate and the only forms available for its descent would be the descendants of the mixed, brute-human species we have been considering. To re-enter earth life in a body far inferior in beauty and purity to the one that was yours in a previous life would have results similar to the experiences of the few unfortunate survivors who first had to endure the mingling of their lives with those of a sub-human race. This is in perfect agreement with what we were saying before about the gradual return into the human race of the earlier type of being fabled as living in lost Atlantis. None of these myths may represent the exact facts of the story, but they all reflect shadows of the true facts and so should not lightly be dismissed.

'The Atlantis story, then gives some support to my reconstruction, as well as the legend of the fall as the Hebrews have it. But I rely also on the contradictions of the evolutionary theory itself. No one could make sense of the Darwinian position as it stood in my day. The human skeleton is unfortunately short lived. The sub-human remains that have been found are not convincing as ancestors of the human in any direct line of descent. Between any of these sub-human forms and Paleolithic man, little as we know of him, there appears to be a tremendous gap. But if we conceive of a true human species of far finer type mingled arbitrarily with a sub-human species then the riddle is on the way to solution. I am not, you see, in a position to try out my theory; it is only an hypothesis which gives, in my opinion, the most economical explanation of all the facts and which might prove fruitful in the field of research. I do not see how the notion could be substantiated by archaeological discoveries, unless by the uncovering of the remains of the original pure human race in such a position that their remote antiquity could not be questioned. If the early race was, as the legend suggests completely overwhelmed and only a few escaped to mix with another breed it is very unlikely that we shall ever happen upon their actual remains. Moreover, there is a hint that their bodies were of a more ethereal kind, which would make preservation still more unlikely. But in spite of these difficulties I have a strong hope that the discovery will some day be made.

'Here I am tempted to be utterly fantastic. Since I came from earth I make many queer guesses at some of the riddles that used to puzzle me. They come in the shape of visions and are as though I myself am acting in them. So I give you this one for what it is worth. I make my way down a silted-up water course in a valley of Asia Minor. Halfway down, I dig through immense levels of silt and then through shale down to harder rock until I come upon the skeletons of a woman and child. I have an impression that I am not far from the fabled site of the Garden of Eden, but this may be mere association. The skeletons are well-preserved and I feel that they lie at a depth of about twenty feet. The ground slopes steeply at this point of the valley; in fact, I see it all so clearly that I feel I could walk straight to the spot. This doesn't help, of course, since I am not in a position to do so. The interesting thing in my picture of the actual skeletons is that the child skeleton is entirely enclosed in a thick cocoon formed of the mother's hair. What that portends I do not know. I do not see how this connects with the Bible story but it may contain hints if the nearness of the Eden site has any significance. So much knowledge is buried in mythology that even a fantastic vision like this might indicate some connection. But I see that our Medium is getting restive. She always does when we introduce matter which, being out of her scope, seems to her fantastic.'

'Unkind,' I said. 'I admit that I am straining to get back to the practical aspect of this admixture idea. I do not like Freud's equally fantastic incest theory based on a notion of the primitive rebellion of sons against the father as an explanation of the guilt complex which seems native to the human mind. If one could find any supporting evidence for this hypothesis of a mixture of advanced and sub-human races it would provide a more self-consistent theory to account for the powerful conflicts in the unconscious mind which are grouped particularly around the sex motive. It seems almost worth while to advance this hypothesis without any archaeological support since it might have great practical value in explaining our deviations from the normal animal mode.'

'I imagine that plenty of support could be found in the field of psychology and also in the study of these widespread myths,' said Scott. 'But I should dearly like to be

able to clinch the matter by finding my pair of skeletons.'

'Come back to the historical possibilities arising out of
the belief in rebirth,' said Scott. 'The uneasy story of
human progress, one race climbing to power over the ruins
of another, seems too chaotic to be reduced to any simple
scheme, but the recurrent birth of its great men, and the
steady return of its slave and subject populations must
surely impose a kind of order on events. We know too little
about the laws of rebirth to dogmatise. We should need
data about the intervals between incarnations, and Andrew who has been here longer than I and can therefore
tell us more, suggests that there are great differences in this
interval. We are supposing that the less developed souls
spend less time here and return to earth at shorter intervals since they are unable to go beyond the astral planes,
and that the more advanced souls who can go higher may
not return to earth for periods extending to two thousand
years. This gives us something to go on. It means that the
genius or the saint may have reappeared only once or twice
in the whole stretch of historic time whereas the humbler
members of the race may have incarnated again and again
during the same period. But this can be only a generalisa-
tion since we know that it is possible for special reasons
that the advanced soul may forego his bliss and return
voluntarily to earth at shorter intervals.
'Considerations that govern the return of the individual
must also be taken into account. E.K. emphasised the pull
of affinity and I think rightly so; but I think the final
form of the self, the ego, pure and stripped of its outer
forms must have a quality of knowledge which gives it
purpose and direction in its return and choice of environ-

ment. At this final stage of being the man can surely recognise his essential weaknesses and needs since he has reached the limits of his development and is thus aware of his final limitations. He must now see clearly what he lacks and what he has to seek for in his next incarnation if he is to make any further progress. There is surely wisdom enough to guide the choice of environment so that the faults incurred in one lifetime may be corrected in the next. Thus a man who lusted for power in his last lifetime can see now the damage it has done to his real being and he will choose to be born again in conditions where this temptation will have less scope; he who once was great will voluntarily choose a humble part and he who was humble will in his turn aspire to be great. Each will look for the kind of experience which will compensate for what he lacks. The poet may come back as the man of action, the soldier as a man of letters, the philsopher as the fool. Every time one returns this tendency to seek for a balance to previous experience will operate. So it would be vain to look for great men to reappear in the same guise. Out of the wisdom they have acquired they will choose for themselves a widely different fate. This is a part of Karma, the self-made fate that governs us all, not only in our entry into human affairs but for the whole course of our lives from birth to death.'

'How then do you think that affinity works,' I asked.

'Great loves, great hatreds, great debts incurred to another on earth, great opportunities lost: all these act as magnets to the soul and bring one back to earth so that the pattern one has begun may be continued or corrected. Karma is never wholly an individual thing. It is bound up with the lives of others and can only be fulfilled in relation to them. So the story of human relationships, tangled and purposeless as it may seem is one's contemporary effort to make a success out of the elements of living with which one failed, or only partially succeeded before.'

'Then every human encounter is significant and part of the continuing design of an age-long existence?'

'Yes, and I sympathise with you when your thoughts fly here and there searching for a larger meaning to many events in your own experience, but we must not stay to conduct an enquiry into our individual pasts just now.

'It is interesting to think that many of the melodramatic heroes of history as well as some who make no small stir in affairs today are probably men who are exercising power for the first time. They needed that particular experience and they have dared its really awful risks. It is certain that they will expiate any misuse of power when they come here and their next life may well be a very humble one. The man of genuine power and authority whose personal weight is so great that he neither needs nor cares to exert it is the man who has learnt the lesson of power in a previous life and knows only too well the dangers of the power lust.

'It is a sound instinct which prompts men to create social institutions which prevent the accumulation of power in any one person's hands. Both the tyrant and his victim would be spared if society could dispense for good with its dictators. The tyrant bears the heavier penalty; the purgation period is terrible for him and nothing nearer to the pains of hell need be imagined. Remember Dives and Lazarus? Dives is accused of nothing but the exercise of power and the possession of wealth. In our modern sense he had not sinned, but there is no escaping the judgement of what one has become. No exterior judgement is necessary; what one *is* is one's doom.'

'Then if this law of compensation has to be considered, there is very little hope of tracing certain waves of thought, or social tendencies in connection with the return of particular groups of people?' I asked.

'Fascinating as it would be to try, I'm afraid the results would be inconclusive. Waves of thought may be widespread in a certain generation because of the raying out of some special influence from spiritual sources, although there is always the chance that other tendencies may be due to traces of past incarnations affecting the unconscious minds of men born at that particular time. Both effects occur, I have no doubt. If we are to speculate, I should like to think that in Renaissance times there was a widespread return to earth of Greek scholars and artists; the time interval does not forbid it and the spirit of the two ages has much in common. It would amuse me very much, too, to be able to show that British statesmen with their notion of world empire had brought back with them the ideals of ancient Rome, and that the great industrial populations of today are the slave populations of former times. You see how plausible such speculations might be? They may be correct but we are not justified in assuming these things since so many factors make for differences in each incarnation and so few for reappearance in the same form.'

'What about this idea of a change of sex?' I said. 'I have read somewhere in this connection that "Man is woman's fate and woman, man's". I suppose this is understandable, in spite of the revulsion of feeling it produces. In seeking to balance the last life and to develop powers then neglected the man might well choose the woman's part in order to develop patience, endurance and adaptability, while the woman, being strong in these will seek for opportunities to become strong, self-reliant, enterprising and brave. If a change of sex does occur then not the great man but his wife may be the outstanding personality in a succeeding age.'

Scott chuckled at this and then went on:

'That satisfies your sense of justice, doesn't it? I have to grant you that it would be an exquisite revenge. Whatever my personal feelings may be—and I grant you the revulsion of feeling—I am bound to see that it is possible. Sex in any case so soon comes to be of less consequence than qualities of mind that I can easily imagine leaving the sense of maleness or femaleness completely behind when one goes higher. It is ceasing to matter greatly to me already.'

'You know, it removes a big grievance against life from my mind. I have always been keenly aware of the injustice of a woman's lot and although I am not clear that I desire such a change for myself I shall rejoice if it is so, merely in the interests of justice,' I said.

'I think it is true to say that sex modifies the etheric and astral mediums but has little influence upon the more spiritual ego-being. As etheric and astral are left behind, so sex may fade out.

'But now come back to the historical aspect, which fascinates me. I am realising what an extraordinary study history would become if we could follow events on both sides of death and trace men through the ages as they re-entered the earth stage and played each time a different part in its story. We should not then put so much emphasis on the progress of mankind as a whole; we should see that it was always composed of the same elements and instead of talking about waves of civilisation with their following reactions into barbarism, we should see going on from age to age a gradual development and education of the basic human material, returning in life after life to learn fresh lessons and to make yet another effort to master its fate. Historians have as yet no notion of the real difficulty of their subject; they will never make the human story con-

209

vincing until they are able to fit the whole thing together instead of trying to make half the causes responsible for all the effects.

'The general effect of the theory of rebirth is to add to the complexity of our knowledge in one way, but to make it more coherent in another. It is like trying to play a game, first with half a pack of cards and then with the whole. In the first case one has less cards to understand and handle but the game simply won't work out; in the second, there are a great many more cards to handle, but the game does work out. While we try to understand the problems of life without the notion of rebirth, hardly any of them admit of a solution; we are constantly left with insufficient data to work with. But when we invoke the theory of rebirth, our knowledge becomes more complex but hitherto insoluble problems now begin to work out.'

Chapter Fifteen

I have probably given the impression that my mediumistic experiences were all of a straightforward character, consisting simply of a series of conversations carried on by means of automatic writing. I think it is impossible to develop the power to make real contacts without laying oneself open to other experiences which are not so easy to understand or describe. I have so far avoided bringing them into this account but now the time has come when the effort to fit them into their proper place in the theory must be made. Perhaps this chapter should be skipped by any reader who is not interested in the more esoteric side of a medium's experiences.

Unusual states of consciousness, a different kind of awareness, do occur. They are usually the result of a long period of study and thought. If any reward is necessary for the vicissitudes of a medium's life one certainly gets it in these brief but radiant glimpses of a happier, fuller kind of living. Such interludes have no likeness to the dream state which is one of lowered vitality and dimmer vision; on the contrary they bring heightened consciousness, keener vision and a clear and joyful emotion. Their after effects are entirely beneficial. There is an immediate reaction of love and understanding and a release of strength. It might be possible to explain them in psychological terms as the resolution of some inward conflict and the consequent release of energy, but having regard to the content of such experiences as I have had I find this explanation inadequate. It looks to me like one of those clumsy generalisations we use to cloak our ignorance.

E.K., with his meditative temperament, helped me most to an understanding of what actually happens on such occasions. He said: 'One might make two mistakes here: the first would be to regard such experiences as purely subjective; the second would be to claim for them objective reality. They are genuine contacts made by your higher self with higher realities, but they are disguised in symbolic form because they have to be interpreted by the brain mechanism tied to a physical body. All experiences which involve the higher self, that is, the astral-ego bodies, must appear to take place *within* you but your ego self is less individualised than the rest of your being and it has affinities with reality of a universal order. By right of this power you can have authentic experiences of universal reality for such time as you can forget your isolated individual self and identify yourself with the universal consciousness of your ego-self. A body-centred mind cuts one off from universal experience but on rare occasions it does become possible to transcend it and then the strength, sweetness and light of another kind of life can flow into the soul. You are thinking of the special experience which we thought must have a cosmic significance?'

'Yes,' I said. 'I had been meditating on the moon-earth relation and had reached the stage when my sense of identity was becoming dim. Suddenly it was as though I was picked up, whirled round and suddenly given the opportunity to fling myself into a different system of movement. This was a hair-raising hazard, but I made the desperate effort that was required and as I did so, I got the vision. It is very hard to describe; I shall only fail if I try to put it into words.'

'Try, nevertheless,' said E.K.

'There were two arcs of shining silver light and they were rapidly approaching each other in space. They were both alive and quivering with power and the sense of swift movement. I thought of powerful circuits of electricity, dangerous and beautiful. If they had collided the clash of such potent forces must have been catastrophic. As they came together they met, not with the direct impact which had seemed inevitable, but sliding harmoniously into relation with each other. It was to be felt that the forces that travelled each circuit were inviolable; they might come into relation but they could not impinge on each other. The intentness of my concentration matched the terrible power in the shining arcs. My life was almost drawn out of me. In the very moment of their meeting and sliding together I was aware that by a great effort, a plunge of re-orientation I had to leap into the opposing system. Somehow I succeeded but only at the utmost stretch of effort and with the loss of my normal consciousness. Yet all this took place in my mind alone; physically I had not moved. The sign that remained with me after this breathless adventure of the mind was that of a shining crescent riding upon an arc of light.'

'There is no doubt that you were being taught something important there, although I think your vision had symbolic rather than actual meaning. What kind of feeling accompanied it?'

'I was exhausted with the queer kind of non-physical effort I had made, but simply radiant with joy, and deeply satisfied as though I had achieved something very important. For some time afterwards I could not get rid of the impression of light playing round my head; a purely subjective impression, of course. I could understand nothing of the meaning of it all. In fact, I have never been able to interpret the thing at all.'

'For me,' said E.K., 'the vision has a direct bearing on cosmic truth, but you will have to revise your ideas of the solar system if you are to follow this. You think of a central sun, an isolated body around which other isolated bodies wander in well known paths, controlled by a force exerted by the greater upon the less; the Newtonian view, in fact. Now forget the heavenly bodies and think instead of their orbits. Try to see each planetary orbit as the rim

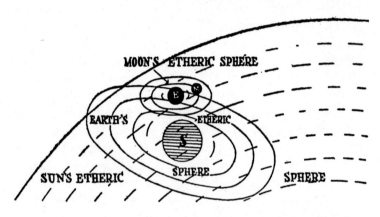

of a great wheel, only the wheel is really a flattened vast hollow disc. The sphere that is visible to you, the ball of the planet, is only a patch of etheric matter, which, for a reason we will discuss later on has become crystallised out into what you call matter. The actual planet as we see it is this great spheroid of ether, the great etheric tract which forms its enclosed orbit and it is this etheric spheroid which revolves in space, carrying around with it on its rim the small physical body you see as the planet. This does not travel unsupported in space and only held in place by some mysterious attraction exerted by the sun; it is a part of the outer edge of a spheroid of ether and its relation to this etheric tract is that of the part to the whole.

214

Caption to diagram.

Many years after the experience here related the vision of the shining arcs took on more specific meaning. Several things came together into meaningful relationship under this symbol, consequent upon the cosmic theory of the earth-spheres and their connection with the larger etheric sphere of the earth's orbit.

In the original vision, the effort demanded of me was to leap from one moving arc to the other, which was inclined to it at an angle. This was rather like transferring from one escalator to another moving rapidly at another angle. These shining tracks, moving with great speed and power were awe-inspiring and much courage was needed to make the effort.

If this was indicative of the angle of the earth's surface to that of the etheric globe and if my communicators are to be understood as inhabiting the latter, comparisons of distance and spatial values naturally present great difficulty, being complicated by mathematical factors of proportional size and tangential movement. The careful time comparisons made by E.K. would also present a complex problem in mathematics.

To come down to an odd personal experience: when taking my friends' writing my usual position is unaltered but on occasions when direct speech takes the place of writing my head is sometimes tilted back as though to look full in the face of someone standing at an angle to my plane of reference. I had accepted this queer experience for years before suddenly realising that it might be explained by the inclined plane of my friends' world.

'Think now of our earth on this plan. It is swept round the sun at the verge of its own etheric disc and at the same time another much smaller disc intersects the larger one. This is the etheric sphere of the moon. These two spheres turn within one another like two interpenetrating wheels.

'Our earth sphere has therefore an interweaving of the two etheric atmospheres, the moon influence being stronger by night and the earth by day. But as your vision suggested, each of these systems of activity is separate and inviolable.

'Now extend your thought to the other planets, each moving with its own sphere of etheric substance and all wheeling round the physical sun. But the system is not self-contained since the sun itself is not at rest. Just as each planet is a particular part of an etheric sphere which fills what you think of as its orbit, so the sun itself wheels through cosmic space around some vaster centre, carrying with it all these interlocked systems of etheric energy. Add to this picture the fact that each etheric system differs in its composition and influence and you will see why the planets may modify our etheric atmosphere, since our path through space takes us into and through many of their etheric fields in turn. Does your vision of these shining tracks through space take on some meaning from this?

'Our view of reality is bound to be different from yours, because the small materialised parts of these etheric systems have ceased to be visible to us. In place of the sun, moon and planets we have their etheric spheres as our basis of reality. I dare not tell you too much now because the idea of such a universe is still strange to you and it will be well not to complicate it with too many details. But forget the illusion of small, solid planets wandering about precariously in empty space. Think rather of those shining discs rotating in harmonious order and mutual dependence, interlocked in a great etheric system and sweeping through the sky on the verge of the stupendous etheric sphere traced out by the sun itself as it rotates through cosmic space about some as yet unknown hub of the universe. The Ancients were feeling for the truth when they spoke of the turning of the spheres; and poets are extraordinary. They say things which can be taken as just pretty expressions, but which we often find are accurate statements of the truth. I wonder what kind of vision was behind Francis Thompson's

> *Not where the wheeling systems darken,*
> *And man's benumbed conceiving soars—'*

'I am staggered by this extraordinary view of the cosmos,' I said to E.K. 'My mind is certainly benumbed and I want time to get it all into focus. It certainly has a terrible beauty, a stability and grandeur far beyond the usual astronomical view. Yet perhaps it does not invalidate the other; it includes it in a vaster whole. Astronomical figures and spaces are impressive, but this vision of the cosmos satisfies the mind and fills those aching spaces.'

'I cannot tell you where in all this vast system of forces you are to look for God,' went on E.K., 'but I can tell you that every one of these spaces is thronged with spiritual beings and that they can pass from sphere to sphere if they have in their composition the right kind of etheric or astral substance. Many of these etheric zones are the homes of spirits or angels, whichever term you prefer. They have no longer any need to enter a physical body. They have reached perfection in some past epoch and now they are pure channels for the will of higher powers. It is likely that there is no physical life as we understand it on these other material planets, but their etheric zones are peopled by spiritual beings of many kinds.'

'I am trying to rid my mind of the notion of empty

217

space and to see the cosmos as a system of interwoven spheres of etheric substance. It is hard to get rid of the idea of impossible empty distances,' I said.

'There is no need to halt at the idea of interstellar spaces. Space in the sense of emptiness is probably an illusion. The network of etheric forces streams everywhere, is linked and woven together so that wherever in this great universe one's spiritual home may be there is always a shining ladder set up between earth and heaven.'

'I want a special way of understanding, a way that is different from an intellectual process, to be able to grasp this idea so that I feel it as reality. I need the kind of understanding that has come to me on rare occasions when, instead of standing outside the thing to be known I become the thing itself and so can know it fully. I see dimly that my vision of the shining arcs was of this nature. Help me to understand what happens when I enter into that state of mind.'

'I think I can give you the proper background for it if you will take it,' said E.K., 'but be docile and receptive and stop trying to *think* about it. Let it come into you and become you.'

'I'll try. Please go on.'

'All these experiences take place within the self and solely in the higher powers of the self. It is as though the ego, which is a universal principle—if it can only act independently of the powers which are tied to your body—has this capacity to become one with the universe; not to *know about* it, as though knower and known were two things, but to be loosed from the individual and set free into the universal mode of experiencing. In your present condition you cannot for long forego the connection with your bodily self so the vision is transient, the experience rare and brief. But whenever consciousness can be lifted to this degree of being it opens out on to the universe and makes you one with whatever is for the moment within your power to apprehend.

'But—and here is the difficulty—the reality is enacted as though it is *within* the self, and not objective to it. This must be so while you are living on a plane of actuality which is below this experience of universality. If all your being were of this one kind, if you had reached the pure ego-quality of the end of your life-cycle, these things, instead of appearing to happen within you, would be part of your normal *outer* experience. They would be your ordinary world of actuality and would appear to take place objectively, in your environment. But while your actual world is the physical world the only way in which you can know the universal spiritual life is as an internal experience—a subjective one, if you like. In reality, it is a setting free of the ego into its proper sphere of universal spirit.'

'May I break in here,' said Scott, 'with a personal experience which bears out what you are saying. Although we have dispensed with a physical body we still have a self-centred consciousness which cuts us off normally from this larger experience. But since I came here so many mystic states of consciousness are possible to me that I frequently fail to understand what I experience.

'It was natural to imagine that after death one would have opportunities of meeting and knowing some of the men whose spirits had influenced me most on earth; poets particularly. I found that most of these had passed on and my only hope was that in course of time I might follow and find them. Often I thought of them and got clear pictures of them as though I could see them in their present state. They were not present in my environment, you understand; and these pictures I took to be subjective. I remem-

219

ber one such occasion vividly. Shelley. Suddenly my mental picture of him began to move; he was trying to find me, we were trying to meet. I gave him directions, since I seemed to know the way by some sense I did not know I possessed. He disappeared from sight but I could feel his ascent as though by a winding staircase and his search for a door which I knew was hidden on the right hand. I felt all this was taking place in my own substance; I was the staircase and the moving figure, I was the one who waited, tense with expectancy; presently I was the ecstasy of joy with which we met and greeted each other. We remained together for some time and the experience was as real to me, as actual, as anything I can hear or see with my present bodily consciousness. I came back to objective life by way of the thought of the immense area my invisible body must fill since all this was taking place within me. This brought me back to my actual surroundings and the vision faded.'

'That is an excellent example of the universal mode of experiencing,' said E.K. 'It depends on identifying the consciousness with the ego-being which alone has this capacity to transcend the limitations of the body. Distance in a spatial sense does not exist for such a mode of experiencing. The only measure of distance is in degrees of affinity. You can reach, or be reached by any thought or any being who is spiritually akin to you since they are always near to you in the world of the spirit.'

'I have always been very suspicious of mystic experiences,' said Scott. 'But if one comes to have some knowledge of the process that causes them and can therefore think of them as normal and possible given the right conditions, one would like to develop the power to use this mode at will.'

'I should advise you to live fully in your present world of actuality which is for the time being your real business.

The opportunities of its contacts and friendships will not come to you again. But at the same time, practise releasing your higher self into the universal life because thus you will strengthen your being, besides finding in such experiences the utmost joy and satisfaction. Now I am inclined to blame J— here, for putting her experiences on one side and making no effort to repeat them.'

'I could not realise their true nature before,' I said. 'I took them as symbols, or prophecies of what might one day be possible, or even as madness.'

'You have to accustom yourself to the view that these are actual happenings in another world of being and that you can have access to that world whenever you can live at that altitude. What have you done about it since? Nothing at all; just buried it.'

'Stop, please, E.K.,' said Scott. 'That is not just. What about the uncanny things that happened after the vision J— has been describing? What about those drawings we none of us understand? What about the help that comes to us from unknown sources when, as now, we are working together?'

'You do well to remind me. Yes, there were glimpses of a lost and forgotten world and of bygone races with which you were identified. Terrible happenings too; earthquakes, great floods, the destruction of ancient cities and visions of lost and wandering survivors of antique civilisations. Well, you see, we are all guessing. Now what?'

'As you know, I shared in some of these terrible experiences,' said Scott. 'They took place in what seemed to have become our common consciousness, yet we were not onlookers but actors in what seemed to be immediate events.'

'Yes,' said E.K. 'Another interesting thing about these visions of a forgotten world is the time factor. What I said about the illusion of space and distance is true also of time. That likewise becomes an illusion when one is existing in the universal world of the spirit. What once was, is, and ever shall be. If you retraced your steps over a past which lies dormant in your unconscious minds, it had to be re-lived as a present reality by the ego, since in this mode time, as divided into past, present and future does not exist.'

'That is harder to grasp than the idea of space being an illusion,' I said. 'Wireless telegraphy has accustomed us to disregard space, but our one-way consciousness makes it very difficult to transcend the idea of time.'

'It will always be so while you set your brain to work on the problem and try so hard to understand it intellectually. There was no difficulty when you *experienced* past, present and future as one,' said E.K.

'You mean that terrifying vision of timelessness which my own inadequacy made so agonising,' I said. 'But a very simple experience convinced me of the illusory nature of *clock* time. One morning I was deep in consideration of a difficult problem and was jotting down notes upon it. The clock was in front of me, the minute hand was at 11.25, and I had a duty to attend to at 11.30. I needed more time and was much disturbed, because to interrupt the thought that was coming to me just then might be to lose it for ever. My pen wrote "Go on. You will be given time". I put the thought of haste out of my mind and went on to finish working out my problem. Another page of notes went down and a conclusion was reached. Free from my pre-occupation I looked up at the clock expecting to find that it was at least twelve o'clock. I sat up with a jerk and rubbed my eyes. The minute hand registered 11.26; one minute only had elapsed. I had indeed been "given time". I felt as though I had gone through a door into a world where the time consciousness did not exist and having lived effortlessly in that world for a long time, had come back through the door to find myself exactly where, in point of time, I had gone out. It is the only time this experience has come to me, though I confess that being a busy woman, I should often have welcomed it.'

'You will only be told that you misread the clock in the first place,' said Scott.

'Naturally, I had that thought myself,' I replied. 'But I had been working to time all the morning and had been following the clock so closely that I cannot think it is likely to have been misread. But for close attention to the time factor I should not necessarily have been aware of the oddity of my experience. As you imply, there can be no confirmation of my story, but I, who had the experience, do not need so much convincing that time is an illusion, and that it is possible to escape from the illusion sometimes.'

Here Andrew joined us.

'You see, J—' he said, 'I, being a practical sort of person rather deprecate these extreme experiences. One has to be a sort of Yogi, or a mystic proper before they can happen to one, and although I have been here some time they don't happen to me and may not do so for some time. My world is a very material one as yet and I should feel lost and antagonised by such a topsy-turvy business as the annihilation of space and time. I grant you that one has to get used to differences in one's consciousness of them but don't get afraid and imagine that one is expected to plunge straight into such eerie experiences.'

'I think this is the explanation that covers it all,' said E.K. 'When one trespasses on the proper experiences of another plane one can only have them subjectively. They lack their proper environment and have to take place in that part of the self which suits the special plane upon which

223

they are realities. This is equally true for us when we reach above our own plane.'

'It is also true for us when we deliberately go down to a lower plane,' said Andrew. 'I was telling you that when we were talking about the work of a guide. One has to put one's body into such a state that consciousness of this plane fades out and one lives interiorly as in a trance or dream. It is just as much a subjective experience for the guide, but in going downwards there is a dimming of consciousness instead of the heightening of awareness you have been describing.'

'I imagine that it also describes the way clairvoyance works for us here,' I said. 'Things must appear to happen within the self. There is certainly that feeling that Scott mentioned, of being boundless, immense, and of great events happening within the scope of the self.'

'Yes, I think we have partly cleared a very difficult business. Strange how pieces of the puzzle we had to discard before have fallen beautifully into place today.'

'I don't think I could have avoided discarding those queer happenings at the time, E.K. I was utterly without any clue to their meaning and could do nothing but put them by. There have been others, equally full of meaning, but a meaning not accessible to me as yet.'

'I did not think I should ever induce you to take that explanation about the cosmos,' said E.K. 'From your point of view I knew you must regard it as fantastic. Yet it was essential for you to have it because it gave meaning to a whole series of things you needed to understand. And the moral of that is, don't trust entirely to an intellectual assessment of things.'

What conclusions can the reader draw from this rather obscure discussion? Only perhaps the notion that there is no dead level of experience to which events of the mind must needs conform; adventures of the heights as well as of the depths have equal claims to authenticity. Yet I must admit that, lacking the special experiences I have hinted at in this chapter I might myself scout such accounts as moonshine and madness, and that a suitable pathological label for their author might not be hard to find.

Chapter Sixteen

'Religious ideas must be strongly affected by the buried memories stored in the ego-being,' I said to E.K. 'After-death experiences, if they leave any trace in the returning soul must surely colour religious beliefs in the ensuing lifetime?'

'In his religious experience man is on tip-toe to reach the stars; he is straining up to grasp the highest thought and emotion with the highest powers of his own being. The effort often lights up again traces of past spiritual experiences and he dreams dreams and sees visions and utters prophecies the origin of which are in the past as well as in the future, since they come out of that timeless world of the spirit which has no past and no future but exists always in the eternity of the present.

'But let us look more closely into some of the typical religions which have taken form out of this timeless eternity in man. Three main urges lie behind the forms of religion: a strong sense of the reality and importance of a super-sensible world; a strong conviction of the survival of some part of the personality after death; and a keen desire to find and understand the spiritual background of life. These urges originate in the astral and ego being. The driving force of desire is turned outward to seek a good not bounded by the personality, a good which can only be grasped by the ego in its universal aspect. When a man follows these deeper urges he must needs, as I said, stand on tip-toe and make his foredoomed grasp at the stars. He can only satisfy his God-hunger and feed his faith in immortality by the use of the highest powers of his own being and in using these he inevitably becomes involved in the universal mode of experiencing which we have just been discussing. Naturally he is bewildered by his experiences and frustrated in his desire to impart them to others. Language, framed to meet the practical issues of daily living, fails him when he enters the authentic religious sphere. He falls back perforce upon symbols. Images, pictures, rites, rhythmic expressions of the unfathomable emotions astir within him have to take the place of language. The religious genius, the prophet, the saint, emerge as typical figures and out of their travail a religion is born.'

'That can be said of all religions with equal truth, perhaps,' I said. 'Yet surely not all religions reflect an equal spiritual truth? How can one account for the primitive and degraded forms of religion, crude animism, totem worship, belief in evil spirits? How is it that man has progressed from these to the higher truths of the great universal faiths?'

'To understand the progression we need to go carefully over the effects of the series of life-cycles which have been lived by each one of us. Cease to think of these benighted primitives of the past as beings of quite another order and see them as the veritable men and women of your own generation living in a past which lives on eternally in your own present. They are yourselves. You are watching the steps of your own progress down the ages.

'Primitive man had an astral being but barely the dawning of an ego-principle. After death his being would hover between the etheric and lower astral and would quickly descend again into a physical body. His highest experiences, then, would be those of the lower astral planes and in many cases no doubt the after-death existence must have been dominated by the animal plane from which he had only just emerged. When such a being went back to earth his vague yearnings for spiritual truth would bring back to him visions of animal forms, of elemental beings of earth, air and water and of the unformed primitive man-soul itself. Fleeting visions of these things would haunt his dreams and he would carve them into his images, symbolise them in his legends and sing them in his songs. But each life cycle would add to his development and enable him to reach a higher plane of existence here. In later lives, when he reached the higher astral planes after death, he would go back to earth with the power to create more beautiful forms, to imagine more beautiful beings and to experience more beautiful emotions. Angels henceforth mingle with the demon and animal symbols of his earlier worship. Heroes and demi-gods, half human, half divine, reflect in his religion the stages of his spiritual experiences up here. Then, still progressing, he reaches the higher spheres and becomes aware of exalted spiritual beings who lead him on to a knowledge of the higher spiritual truths and set him hungering to find and worship the supreme spirit.

'When he comes back to earth the kingdom, the power and the glory of his heritage will be present in his inner being and he will know the hunger of the soul which cannot be satisfied by even the most wonderful experiences of earthly life. So his hunger, his urge to find again the pure joy once known by him here will influence his religious thought and will purify and ennoble the form of religion he finds as his inheritance on earth. If he has gone far here so that he brings back to earth a pure thought of God, his inner knowledge may lead him into rebellion against the state of religious thought he finds on earth. He may become a great heretic, a great reformer; but such a heretic is the saint of the future. The vision is always with him, the kingdom of heaven is within him. Earthly religious forms carrying the outworn symbols and images of a more primitive past must, for him, be purged and lifted on to a more enlightened level of spiritual truth. The connection with evolution becomes plain. But for this perpetual reaching up to the highest possible to man in each lifetime there could be no progress since no higher plane can be reached here unless the power to reach it has been developed on earth. The earth experience is decisive and controls the rest of that cycle and the plane to which ascent can be made.'

'Psychologists have been inclined to attribute the religious instinct to a diversion of the libido usually concerned with sex, what they call a sublimation of the sexual urge. What do you think of this?' I asked.

'I think it nonsense,' said E.K. 'The sex motive is an urge that affects the physical, etheric and astral bodies. The etheric and astral are about equally concerned in it and the physical is simply their tool. The ego stands somewhat aloof, except in unions where there is shared ego-experience in the past and then the quality of the love between the two takes on an almost religious tone. This for good reason, since the highest spiritual faculties are involved in it. Then it is an ego tie as well as an astral-etheric union. But in the true religious experience the ego is primarily the active agent and although it may stimulate and use the astral being as well, the religious urge is really a spiritual need to rediscover the love and joy and peace of the home of the spirit from which the ego feels itself in exile.'

'I suppose the chaos in psychology is largely due to ignorance of the existence and special powers of the four principles of the human body, for if every activity has to be accounted for by glands, secretions and reflexes muddle and contradictions are inevitable. It is as though the glass and the mercury backing of a mirror had to be accountable for all that moves in the mirror. An English psychologist has stated that the religious motive comes directly from projections of the mother and father images and then he goes on to argue from his own cases that no one can be mentally healthy unless he has a satisfying religious faith. This implies that we must in our own interests become either fools or knaves. We must be genuinely duped by our projections or we must profess a faith in them which we know to be a delusion.'

'I am glad that I can give you better grounds for a religious faith than that,' said E.K. 'While the ego remembers it will always be hungering and thirsting for the joys it once knew and a careful examination of religious systems of both past and present will easily uncover the connection between such a hidden memory and its projection in symbol and rite. I am not afraid of that word projection. It describes exactly what happens when the buried unconscious memory casts a shadow upon consciousness making there an image which may well be distorted and larger than life but which will still retain some likeness to its origin in far-off spiritual experience.'

'I am thinking that the projection of this hidden trace of our highest spiritual experience may also be embodied in our ideas of heaven. There have been many versions of paradise in different religions,' I said.

'And all of them reflect equal truth when one comes to trace their origin,' said E.K. 'Their differences are due to their reflection of the various spiritual planes; "many mansions", as Christ told us. Earliest come the ideas of lost and wandering souls, the wailing wraiths of Hades, the sorrowful shadows of Sheol. These are probably reflections of the etheric world, the "no-man's land" of which

Scott had such an eerie experience. Later we find these giving place to more concrete heavens, Valhallas and Paradises which are very like an idealised earth life. These are traces of the astral worlds. The higher planes are reflected in visions of the New Jerusalem and in the Christian Heaven, but I think that the highest planes of universal spiritual being are suggested by the Buddhist Nirvana, often mistakenly regarded as loss of being when it is really the most joyful and marvellous experience of the human soul at the peak of its development. But I see that your inveterate habit of making diagrams is combining these stages into a formal shape.'

'Yes, I see it as a reciprocating current, something like this,' I said.

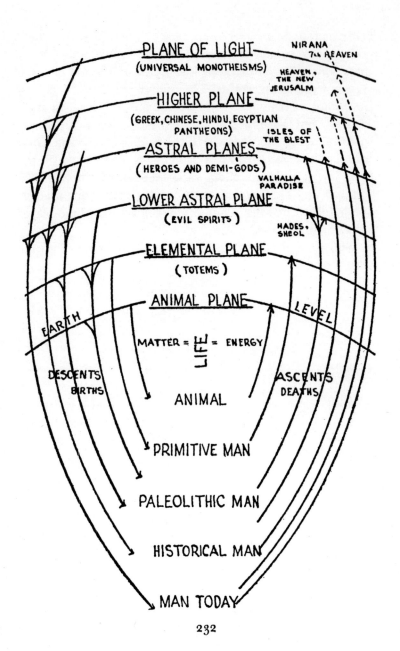

PLANE OF LIGHT
(UNIVERSAL MONOTHEISMS)

NIRANA
7th HEAVEN

HEAVEN,
THE NEW
JERUSALM

HIGHER PLANE
(GREEK, CHINESE, HINDU, EGYPTIAN PANTHEONS)

ISLES OF
THE BLEST

ASTRAL PLANES
(HEROES AND DEMI-GODS)

VALHALLA
PARADISE

LOWER ASTRAL PLANE
(EVIL SPIRITS)

HADES,
SHEOL

ELEMENTAL PLANE
(TOTEMS)

ANIMAL PLANE

LEVEL

EARTH

MATTER = LIFE = ENERGY

DESCENTS
BIRTHS

ASCENTS
DEATHS

ANIMAL

PRIMITIVE MAN

PALEOLITHIC MAN

HISTORICAL MAN

MAN TODAY

Note to diagram:

(*a*) O marks the possible origin of life on the earth level. The first cycle shows it as animal in form, returning at death into the animal plane. Endless ages, and an endless number of descents are summarised in this one cycle.

(*b*) Shows descent from the elemental plane into primitive man, and up again to reach the lower astral; again, a matter of aeons of time and many descents to earth.

(*c*) Shows descent from the astral planes to early man, and his return to still higher planes. Again, many ascents and descents are shown as one.

(*d*) Brings us to historic man, the more advanced members of whom come from higher planes and begin to exhibit the dawning of the ego-principle by means of which they can go still higher.

(*e*) Last, modern man, who may come from the highest planes, or from any of the low or intermediate ones, unfortunately, and who may be capable at the end of this cycle of attaining to the highest plane, the sphere of light shown in the diagram.

But note:

All plane divisions are symbolical only; the spiritual world is by no means so simple as this diagram suggests. Height, as usual, means nothing, since all the planes are inter-spaced with each other and with earth. Evolutionary time, too, is out of all proportion, the earlier periods being immensely longer than historical time.

E.K. added this further note:

'The process by which the human ego has been reached is clear from a study of the diagram. Each earth life forced the astral body into fuller development until at last, in primitive times came the first indications of the dawning ego being. This began as a faint awareness of man's own being as separate from the environment. In lifetime after lifetime this awareness brightened so that man began to know himself as an emotional being increasingly conscious of his own desires and savouring keenly both his joys and his sorrows. Lastly, the ego becomes conscious of itself and man has become a living soul.

'It is to this stage that our many-gathered earth experiences have brought us and as the process continues the ego will establish its mastery over the emotions (astral body) over the sensations (etheric body) and even over the physical body. When this long, slow conquest is accomplished man will begin to live the life of the spirit even on earth. To this we are tending but we have many evil desires and blind and brutal beliefs to shed before we can make further progress.'

'And religious forms,' I asked; 'how do you think they will be affected by this better quality of consciousness?'

'Remember that *all* religions are true religions as long as they suit the stage of development of the race that holds them. A *false* religion was once true; it has been outgrown and needs to be superseded,' said E.K. 'False elements in religion are these same outgrown phases which cling on to the living and growing faith. Actually the truest form of a religion is the one to which we can hardly reach, the one to which we are growing. Christianity as its founder preached it, is such a faith. It will take us many ages yet to reach it. All the accretions and elaborations men have added to it to make it easier will have

234

to be shed. Even in one lifetime we can make great progress in this search for a truer truth than satisfies us in youth.

'I have emphasised the human striving after truth because nothing can become true for you until you are capable of seeing it. But there is the other side. Spiritual beings are always at work trying deliberately to reach your understanding and to influence your thought. The ego-consciousness is still in its infancy but as it develops more fully it will make us more sensitive to these influences and so the process will accelerate. Men will come to have, as part of their normal experience a real awareness of the spiritual world and what becomes a part of actual experience will demand to be understood and ranged justly with other knowledge. So theory will have to keep pace with practice, and your longed-for consummation of the linking of science with spiritual truth will come to pass. You may not see it in your present lifetime but when next you come back to earth much of what I am prophesying will have come to pass. From both sides the psychic bridge will have been built and men will be passing freely and safely across it while we, on this side, shall be able to reach you and make a way for the full invasion of the spiritual into the normal life of earth.'

We had been talking of the arbitrary division between good and evil and E.K. went on to give what I felt to be a valuable analysis. He said:

'To search out the beginnings of this deep problem I have to take you back aeons of time to an epoch of cosmic history before our universe took shape. As a result of a long period of evolution a race of pure beings emerged who were thus able to find a permanent home in the lovely world of light which is nearest to the sphere of the Highest.

Creative love itself could enter them and possess them fully and could use them freely as channels for its will. But this vanished epoch closed before the whole of the race could be thus perfected; some of its members lagged behind and so found themselves in conflict with the spiritual world. Thus there developed a spirit of opposition to the Will of God and it found special manifestation in certain localised parts of the astral and etheric universe. Wherever this conflict raged, the light of the spiritual world was turned to darkness; thus, in these areas of strife we see nothingness and you see the visible sun, moon, planets and stars. In each of the great spheres of etheric activity which fill the universe with their inter-related systems, we spoke of the material orb as being only a small part of the larger spiritual entity. In other words, the orb of matter is the localised scene of strife in each etheric sphere. So, wherever matter has been precipitated out of the surrounding etheric substance, it is the result of this conflict—it is a sign of the interlocking there of two forces, one the power of Creative Love, the other a principle of opposing chaos felt as inertia.

'When first this struggle began there was only chaos, the world without form and void, you remember. The outward sign of conflict, which is the presence of matter, was there, but it had no form nor cohesion. Then the irresistible influence of Creativity, the insistence of God's thought and purpose began to over-rule the strife and to impose the first form of order and pattern upon formless energy. "The Spirit of God brooded over the face of the waters," we are told, and since spiritual night had fallen on that part of the universe light in a physical form had to be re-created. The very radiations given out from the regions of strife themselves became that light, yet it is only an illusion of the light of reality. "Let there be light" actually means that the beings who should inhabit these spheres of matter must be so adapted to spiritual darkness that they would evolve the kind of sense organs which responded to physical stimulus as though it were indeed light. The word "light" could have no meaning until creatures should be created with eyes which would so interpret the rays streaming out from the material sun.

'Let us return to the strife between the two spiritual forces which caused matter to crystallise out from the surrounding ether. You remember when we were discussing the atom with its concentric systems of activity vibrating about a nucleus we came on the axiom that none of this activity could be manifest unless it were shown to us, as it were, by opposition. We saw that any force operating in a perfect vacuum would spend itself invisibly, intangibly since there would be nothing to record its passage through space. Hence if the atom were nothing but a system of activity we must admit that it could be neither felt nor known by us unless it were in the process of overcoming resistance. Two questions arise out of this: first, why is the system of activity which is the foundation of matter visible to us and secondly, why does this activity take ordered forms?

'To answer the first question, we have to postulate a principle of opposition, and since this is not immediately discoverable by the methods of science, it becomes probable that it operates in a medium which, while linked with matter is not yet within the scope of scientific discovery. We know this medium as the etheric activity upon which matter is based. In answer to the second question, we assert that this order is imposed on chaotic strife by the will and purpose of God who is invoked as the Principle of Order and Harmony and described in human terms as Creative Love. For there is really no justification for an *a priori* assumption of the necessity for the order and rhythm found in nature. *Why* order, unless the guiding principle of the universe is of this nature in itself?

'The story of creation is the gradual conquest of chaos by the thought and purpose of God. Every natural object, from the atom to the farthest star, is a pattern formed out of mere senseless strife, a rhythm imposed upon purposeless energy. Now that science is uncovering some of the secrets of atomic structure it begins to appear that the patterns which emerge are similar, whether we examine a solar system with planets circling the sun, or an atom with electrons circling a nucleus. But what I have said about planets—that they are parts of an etheric system which has crystallised out locally into matter and that a solar system is really a great interweaving of etheric spheres may well be the truth about the smaller universe of the atom. For electrons are not particles, they are waves; they are perhaps formed on the same model as the cosmos itself and may prove to be just such a system of interlocking etheric spheres of activity. Is this why they sometimes appear to be particles and another time waves? We may note, too, the extreme difficulty of dislocating these tiny universes. Immense power is needed to tear them apart and their stability is well accounted for by this hypothesis.

'Creation begins, then, as a scene of strife wherein certain powers acted in opposition to the rest of the spiritual world. Regions of neutralised spiritual substance resulted where these two forces were interlocked. Here was the original chaos. But beyond and around the small spheres of strife is the immense world of the spirit where the timeless principle of Creative Love, the great formative spirit of God rules without opposition. Into the regions of chaos and old night this influence streamed and by slow degrees chaos had to yield to creativity. The mere disorder of elemental strife gave way as orderly rhythms and grouping overtook its jangled vibrations and organised them into ever larger and more complex designs. This work of creation has never stopped; it is still overruling strife and disorder and producing new and more intricate forms of order. We call this evolution, and having given creation a new name think that we have abolished the need for a Creator. But we have only to ask ourselves why order and design should emerge at all and why there should be in evolution this upward trend towards ever more intricate and delicate harmonies to realise that we still need to postulate a purpose and a principle of harmony to account for the order we see in the world. It is very little that you see on earth, but that little is enough and such a conclusion is amply confirmed by all that we see and know of life here.

'It has an inevitability, this slow gathering of order upon order, this mustering of energy, first in simple patterns and then in combination to form larger and more complex designs. It is obvious, too, that the process need have no end and that it cannot be deferred or defeated. In our short span of earth life, when time and space condition our thought and limit our understanding, we see the world as static, finished, given over to strife; but even one step out of the arena of conflict, just the one step out of the body that we take at death, gives us a different view, a larger understanding. The theory at which we have been working shows clearly the process of evolution at work upon matter. The patterns of activity which formed matter were elaborated until a new *form* of energy emerged and the creative thought of God thus produced the first forms of life. The surrounding ether was able to combine with this new form of activity and the dark world of non-being which is matter, began to be penetrated by the dim etheric glow wherever living forms established themselves. Etheric activity then produced an accelerated vibration which gave rise to more advanced forms of order. The single-celled creature elaborated until the world was filled with a bewildering variety of organisms. Then another kind of activity began to emerge. Pleasure, pain and desire working towards new purpose were the signs of another mode of being, and the power to feel emotions meant that the astral form was emerging from the etheric and was drawing astral substance from the spiritual world. In our own case, the latest triumph of creativity has been the emergence of the ego, the spiritual form of activity which at last restores our kinship with the Creator himself.

'Each of these stages in the ascent of life represents a triumph of the spiritual over the material realm so that the spiritual may re-enter it. Three times the triumph has been repeated: first when matter reached a state when the etheric could enter and produce life; next when the etheric and the physical body reached a sufficient complexity to create the right conditions for the entry of the astral; and last, when the animal organism thus created reached a stage of complexity, of heightened activity, so that the ego spirit could combine with it. But do not suppose that this is final in the story of creation. Why indeed should it be so?

'I want you to see now that every stage of creativity has been contested by the original principle of opposition. Just as the Creative Love of God has triumphed at each stage and has produced a new form of being more free from the inertness of matter and nearer to the life of the spirit, so the principle of opposition, of strife and disorder has followed the new creation into the new plane of being. Each new Eden has been in turn invaded by the old serpent. The earth and its etheric and astral planes are the great arena of this cosmic strife. But when we speak of it as a war between Good and Evil we are over-simplifying the issue and using two terms we cannot define. We do not know fully what is good and what is evil.

'It is very clear that these opposing forces have their rightful part to play in human evolution and that without the conflict between them it might never have been possible to create the conditions necessary for the entry of spiritual being into a material universe. The discipline of a material body and environment alone could have forced activity up the steep path of evolution. We have to come down again and again into the material world so that its difficulties and dangers may temper and refine the fourfold body of man.

'Let us understand the real nature of the issue. It is not to be thought of as a fight between good and evil, but as a necessary balance of the opposing forces of order and disorder; of creativity and destruction; of love and its nega-tion. In fact, the two poles of existence, the positive and the negative are necessary to the existence of every entity whether it is of matter alone; or of matter and the etheric, as in the plant; of matter, etheric and astral as in the animal; or of matter, etheric, astral and ego as in man. The balance must be there and the two poles of being are evident in each type.

'When we speak of evil in the world, of evil men, evil conditions, evil emotions, we are describing a state of affairs where the negative has overbalanced the positive and where the tendency is towards strife, destruction and disintegration. Whenever the negative gains the ascendant, the trend becomes *self-destructive*; in its very nature evil can only produce more and worse evil and so hastens its own end. This end is always disintegration. The balance has been lost and as it swings over, so it gets nearer to non-being. Whether we see it in matter, living beings, societies, or in the individual, the unbalanced system of activity is doomed to death unless the balance can be readjusted and order and creativity regain the ascendency. But even disintegration is not the end. The positive powers begin again to rebuild out of the ruins a new creation and so justify the ways of God to men. Creativity is never finally defeated. It uses even the outbreaks of disorder to produce more subtle triumphs of order.

'I suppose that if the Principle of Order were to withdraw from the strife in matter, the whole material universe would collapse into ruins and be given over to the reign of chaos. But such a course would be a contradiction in the very nature of God who, being pure love cannot act other than creatively. I see dimly that by way of the gradual conquest of strife there is the possibility of a final triumph over the forces of opposition, an infiltration of spiritual life into matter until creativity alone remains and matter, the outcome of the conflict, fades out of existence altogether. Then the spiritual world will flood back into the realm of matter and claim it for its own. Man is the instrument God has shaped to this end. He is the destined channel through which alone the re-entry of the spiritual can be made.'

Chapter Seventeen

'Let us look now not at the creation of worlds, but of the individual. God "Took of the dust of the earth" and created man. That is true. It happened over long ages of evolutionary time and the end of the statement, that God breathed into His creation the breath of His own nostrils and so man became a living soul refers to the later period when the ego spirit at last entered and began to control man. The process is still going on but now the ego has to work back into the more material principles of the body and gradually penetrate and spiritualise them.

'On earth history is told as the story of the progress of mankind and you are confused by the fact that improvements in the human breed are seldom handed down by way of inheritance. Only the physical form is modified by these means. The creation of a personality is a far more wonderful thing and it is ludicrous to imagine that physical generation and one short lifetime of experience can possibly produce such an astoundingly complex thing. Look for a moment at the long effort of creativity which has brought it out of the night of matter. God, knowing no bounds of time or space, Himself diffused equally throughout the universe could only segregate His own being and create separate living units with the help of the alien principle of matter. So He begins to work on matter; the first day of creation dawns. By imposing order upon strife it becomes possible for etheric matter to combine with matter and life begins in the humble form of single-celled organisms. The act of creating a separate living thing within the world of matter has been accomplished. The second day of creation follows. The organism develops, elaborates and is built up into astonishing forms of intricate order and rhythm. It becomes aware of its environment and is made ready to receive the next principle of being, the astral. This stage is long, but at last sufficient sensitivity is reached to admit the ego principle. So by building up the developing stages of the living creature God can at last give back to it His own being and the personality of man has climbed from the dust into possession of its fourfold being, the highest principle of which brings it into living relation with the Creative Purpose of God. Having climbed this ladder man has now, rung by rung, to destroy it behind him so that he need no longer descend it on to earth again.

'First his spirit must be cleansed from strife and become pure in its proper nature of creative love. Then it must purify the emotional being also until the astral body is spiritualised and last of all, the same process must effectively change the very elements of his gross physical body. When this has been done the purpose of this earth stage of creation may have been achieved and the spirit be finally free from the necessity of descent into matter.

'No series of physical generation could bring this to pass. Progress in the spiritual quality of human life depends on another method of generation by which the individual inherits the nature and stored meaning of his own long series of lives on earth. Unless the same being had essayed earth conditions repeatedly no progress would be possible. The man of genius does not beget genius in his sons. The richness of personality achieved during each lifetime would be wasted if its preservation depended on earthly generation since no man can pass on to his children the quality and meaning of his enriched personality. That remains an inalienable part of himself; in life he cannot transmit it, but it remains the essential part of his being after death.

'If this meaning-quality of a man's life were to be utterly lost the story of mankind could be nothing but the bungling, confused repetition of his original mistakes. But the worth of mankind in terms of meaning has increased and continues to do so since no jot of meaning can be lost. It is the eternal part of the being which is always safe in the keeping of God, who sends it back repeatedly to gather added meaning and to enrich and ennoble itself by another lifetime of earthly experience. If this vast and beautiful view of life is held, where now are good and evil? They are seen as childish terms, expressing half-truths, over-simplified into silliness, but our part as individuals is clear enough. We know the protagonists in the struggle and effort of the ages through which we ourselves have passed. God, versus the Devil; order, versus disorder; harmony, versus strife. We can consciously range ourselves on which side we please. Not for long shall we have the excuse of ignorance, nor shall we for long confuse means with ends. If we are consciously on the side of Creative Love we shall not be able to delude ourselves into thinking that strife and destruction can ever be justified in the pursuit of what we see as righteous ends. It is only a childish mind that can seriously accept the term, "righteous war" for instance, since this is to claim that God can be made to serve the devil.

'Our worst danger is this same childishness and refusal to face honestly the moral facts of life. We hoodwink the ego being and see with our astral sense, by way of our emotions. Wishful thinking motivated by undesirable emotions like anger, envy, cruelty and greed are modes of thinking in which the ego is made the slave of the astral being; it has to break free and to gain control of the emotions.

'You begin to see that the human race is indeed at a crisis of its fateful part in the ancient strife. Faith in matter and in physical force which characterise the age you live in and which finds its logical expression in war, is ranging man on the side of destruction and death. The very sense of justice may be made to serve the ancient adversary and used to legalise murder. But it is idle to imagine that God can be defeated. Having learnt on earth the futility of the creed of matter we pass through death and come here to perfect our lesson by fuller knowledge of the power and glory of the spiritual world. When we come again to earth we shall bring that knowledge with us, not in the form of intellectual concept, but as the inherent bias of our whole character. On our return we shall deal with the inheritance the intervening ages have left us and this deep instinctive knowledge will provide the inspiration by which we shall modify the religious and moral systems of the future. Thoughts of the future and of our necessary part therein bring the time factor back into prominence. We have to take a long view of our recurring appearances upon earth. Let us look at the path that stretches ahead.

'When the ego entered man it brought the very light of God into the dark conflict of matter. It turns that light upon the fourfold body which is rooted in the very matter resulting from conflict and bids man know that his whole being has to be redeemed from strife and made fit to enter the spiritual world. His immediate task is to spiritualise the astral body, which, in moral terms, means to bring the emotions completely under the control of an ego which serves only the purposes of Creative Love. This is an immense task; it will need more than one lifetime for its accomplishment. Then the living power of the etheric body has to be cleared of strife. Suffering and disease will then lessen and in time cease altogether since they originate in the astral and etheric bodies. Last of all, the physical, that obdurate material thing has to be completely spiritualised and if you have followed my thought so far you will realise that when this stage is completed matter can be dispensed with since at last "this corruptible will have put on incorruptibility", and death will be merely transition into another plane of being, no more to be feared than the change from one plane to another as we experience it here.

'Thus the ancient conflict which begot matter is to be resolved by man in his own body. "The seed of the woman shall bruise the serpent's head." If you have any idea of the immensity of the task which is thus set for the human race to accomplish you will realise that all this is aeons away in time. When it comes to pass, the earth may indeed pass away, since all life will have lifted clear of the earth plane and death will be no more. Scientists think that the earth will support life for many millions of years before final entropy overtakes matter and all activity is paralysed in universal death. We are inclined to say: "Oh, it will last my time". But we forget that it has to last until the immense task of spiritualisation is complete for everyone. We ourselves shall need to make many more descents to earth before we have reached this goal. Let us think again; it is surely an open question whether the earth *will* last our time, since our time may well be the whole of earth duration and not the few years of one incarnation.

'I myself am convinced that there is need for haste. The redemption from matter has to be finished for even the most degraded among us or the consequences of that failure will pass over into a new era of cosmic history. The serpent will creep again into a new Eden as he did at the beginning of our present era and the sorrow and suffering of a long redemption from matter will have to be continued upon another stage. This is why we are always being impressed with the need for haste and here is the reason for the urgency with which we seek to impress on you all you can understand of the vast spiritual world, and of our responsibility for the salvation of human kind. Here, too, is the warrant for our grief over the insane waste and hindrance of war. Man seems to us to have reached a dark and dangerous stage in his development; yet the crisis is full of hope for the future if he can only be got to understand the grandeur of the fate he is imperilling by his blind faith in illusions of physical force. The old faiths are dying or dead; their power to illumine the path ahead of mankind and to save him from his tragic ignorance, has gone. The Christian faith needs to be restated in the light of our knowledge as well as of yours and in God's good time the proof of the assumptions we ask you to make will be found.'

'I need to be able to relate what you have told me to Christianity,' I said to E.K. 'I realise that Christians are only a part of the human race and that there must be many more ladders to heaven than our own familiar faith. But for us who have been conditioned from infancy by its teachings Christianity must surely be the way. What can you tell us of Christ and of his influence on your planes?'

'We spoke before of the help given to the individual soul by the Christ Spirit. His coming to earth was a mighty event in the history of mankind. That such a spirit could use a human body at all was wonderful enough and occult teaching has always said that a very special bodily form had to be prepared to that end. A wise and ancient being who often before had been a spiritual leader of mankind came back to earth in the Jewish race and built up a highly-developed astral and ego body. Thus a rare and beautiful

248

soul in an exceptionally ethereal body grew up in the solitudes of Galilee.

'By the time he reached maturity he had attained full knowledge of the great work he was fated to perform. At the height of this realisation he was approached and possessed at the Baptism by a mighty spirit whose influence over our earth had been increasing steadily during the whole of historic time. This great Being had been felt and worshipped under many different names by the races of mankind. His nature and purpose had been particularly realised by the Jewish people who, in their sacred literature, recorded what they understood of his dealings with their race. He drew near now to this particular race and in the pure and beautiful manhood of Jesus of Nazareth he was able to find a vehicle for his work among men. For three years he walked the dusty plane of earth in a physical body which in spite of its fineness and purity was probably unable to contain such a mighty spirit without becoming tenuous and physically frail. This is suggested by the swiftness with which it died under the torture of the Cross.

'But the significance of his descent is clear. By deliberately imprisoning himself in the flesh, he descended into the actual conflict out of which matter is begotten that by so doing he might meet the ancient enemy on his own battlefield. So for evermore he bears within himself the full knowledge of the sorrowful, valiant life of the flesh. In his life upon earth he manifested the power, the spirit and the method of God in his dealings with mankind. Love was the spirit, the power and the method. In himself, he was a portent of the future of man, the prefiguring of the stature of the full manhood to which we all have to attain.

'The Christ Spirit, freed by the cross from the body of Jesus hovered near the earth plane for some time. He has remained ever since identified with our earth plane, sharing its spiritual experiences, influencing its people and seeking and using men to give his message. He helps, inspires and teaches us, not only by the scanty records of his earthly mission but by the continuing presence of his love among men. His mission of hastening the kingdom of God is not completed; it awaits the perfecting of every human soul. "The kingdom of God is within you" he taught, and it is this kingdom of God which has to come into full possession of the whole being of men. Then the work of redemption will be finished. Until then he remains with us. "Lo, I am with you always, even until the end of the earth" is his literal promise. He stays with the human race until the last soul is redeemed from its necessitous return into matter. You will find the gospels themselves build up this truth. It is only in the accretions of Jewish, Greek and Roman thought that Christianity has gone astray. It still bears at its heart the vital truths which have redemptive value because in the teaching of Jesus Christ our recall to the Kingdom of God is sounded clearly for the whole race of men.

'It is our everyday experience here that the influence of the Christ spirit should be constantly felt and we know that it must also stream continually into the darkness of the earth sphere. Wherever the life and thought of men is raised to moral and spiritual heights there a way is made for his power to be felt. In terms of light, wherever the inner light of God glows forth in a man it attracts and absorbs the spiritual light of the higher planes. Affinity with the spirit of Christ assures us that we shall feel his presence. "Wherever two or three are gathered together in my name, there am I in the midst." If we held our Meetings for Worship in the spirit of love the Christ spirit would inevitably be drawn to them and his inspiration and presence would be there in the midst. The nearer we, as individuals, come to his pure and loving spirit the more his strength can flow into us and the greater his likeness in us will become.

'When violence reigns, as in a period of war, the coming of the kingdom is immeasurably hindered. We speak glibly of crucifying Christ afresh; who can know the agony of spiritual suffering we inflict on him at such times? By the awful deeds of war a great total of evil and suffering is piled up by mankind which has all to be purged away. The individual soul, with its special load of guilt may need more than one additional lifetime to make good its loss of development; the purgation period will be lengthened and the whole process of redemption slowed up. But there is nevertheless a mysterious over-ruling in these matters. Evil *is* self-destructive and in order that it may thus destroy itself it seems sometimes to be necessary that it should fully declare itself. Thus a blind faith in matter must be cured by allowing it to work out to its logical conclusion. The toys of matter upon which modern man builds his life and faith must even be allowed to destroy him and his ordered world so that the evil faith may be known for what it is. An outbreak of evil that vents itself and works out to its ultimate futility may even cleanse the body of life for future generations. See how it gathers and breaks in wave after wave throughout history, subsiding and superseded by the order and simplicity of happy human experience.

'However this may be, there will always be a vast sum of suffering accumulated by war of which the least part will be the suffering you see on earth. Here we see the other side of the picture. All those who have *inflicted* suffering will in the after-life experience that suffering in their own being, not as a punishment but as a purgation, since in no other way can they free themselves of their own evil and pass on to a purer life. Not the victim, but the tyrant is to be pitied in the future of his acts.

'So here is the conclusion of the matter.

'In the beginning was the Word, the very meaning and purpose of God, which permeated chaos, ordered it, and gave it meaning. Out of this harmonising process came the whole succession of living beings, culminating in man, who, by the acquisition of the ego became a living soul. This living soul has to redeem every principle of his four-fold body from the dominion of chaos and strife and hence from its need to return into matter. Finally, the whole being of man has to achieve complete spirituality and reunion with its source and origin in God. The agelong cycle of birth and death and return into matter must be continued until the life of the spirit finally emancipates itself from matter. This is not a mere repetition, a return to God of the original spark of spirit. It is the means of creating a mature spiritual being who out of conflict, out of darkness, out of suffering and joy will return as a full grown son of God.

'To this end the thought of God, which is the Creative Love itself, floods urgently into His creation, inspiring, ordering, harmonising, and over-ruling conflict, and in this we have the continuous work of creation we call evolution. To this end, spiritual beings also work cease-lessly, striving to impress upon mankind the meanings and mysteries of the world of reality in which they have their eternal being. To this end the Christ Spirit toils on and suffers with us men in a tireless redemptive effort, seeking to lead us by his own law of love into communion with the Creative Love he himself serves.

'To this end we are to live fully, hopefully, lovingly, courageously, opening ourselves to the light, joy and love of the spiritual realms and living and working either here or on earth up to the limits of our developing powers, remembering that it is our service to render back to God in the form of a mature and perfected being that thought from His own Creative Love of which each of us is an unique expression.

'Let us pray the old prayer with new intention:

'*Thy Kingdom come on earth, as it is in Heaven.*'

Index

256